Catholic Identity School Edition

Sadlier

We•Believe™

Jesus Shares God's Life

WITH PROJECT DISCIPLE

Pray
Learn
Celebrate
Share
Choose
Live

Grade Two

Sadlier

This advanced publication copy has been printed prior to final publication and pending ecclesiastical approval.

Acknowledgments

Excerpts from the English translation of _The Roman Missal_, © 2010, International Committee on English in the Liturgy, Inc. All rights reserved.

Excerpts from the English translation of the _Catechism of the Catholic Church_ for the United States of America, copyright © 1994, United States Catholic Conference, Inc.—Libreria Editrice Vaticana. English translation of the _Catechism of the Catholic Church: Modifications from the Editio Typica_ copyright © 1997, United States Catholic Conference, Inc.—Libreria Editrice Vaticana. Used with permission.

Scripture excerpts are taken from the _New American Bible_ with _Revised New Testament and Psalms_ Copyright © 1991, 1986, 1970, Confraternity of Christian Doctrine, Inc., Washington, D.C. Used with permission. All rights reserved. No part of the _New American Bible_ may be reproduced by any means without permission in writing from the copyright owner.

Excerpts from the English translation of _Lectionary for Mass_ © 1969, 1981, ICEL; excerpts from the English translation of _Rite of Holy Week_ © 1972, ICEL; excerpts from the English translation of the _Rite of Penance_ © 1974, ICEL; excerpts from the English translation of _Eucharistic Prayers for Masses of Reconciliation_ © 1975, ICEL; excerpts from the English translation of _Pastoral Care of the Sick: Rites of Anointing and Viaticum_ © 1982, ICEL; excerpts from the English translation of _A Book of Prayers_ © 1982, ICEL; All rights reserved.

Excerpts from _Catholic Household Blessings and Prayers (Revised Edition)_ copyright © 2007, 1988 United States Catholic Conference, Inc. Washington, D.C. Used with permission. All rights reserved.

English translation of the Lord's Prayer, Glory Be to the Father, and the Apostles' Creed by the International Consultation on English Texts. (ICET)

Excerpt from the Angelus message of Pope Francis, September 1, 2013, and from his _Evangelii Gaudium, Apostolic Exhortation on the Proclamation of the Gospel in Today's World_, November 24, 2013, copyright © Vatican Publishing House, Libreria Editrice Vaticana.

Excerpt from _Pacem in terris, Peace on Earth_, Encyclical Letter, Pope John XXIII, April 11, 1963.

Excerpt from _Lumen Gentium, Dogmatic Constitution on the Church_, Pope Paul VI, November 21, 1964.

Excerpt from Litany of God the Father, _Treasures Old and New: Traditional Prayers for Today's Catholics_, copyright © 2009 Philip Neri Powell, OP, Liguori Publications.

Excerpt from _Unitatis Redintegratio, Decree on Ecumenism_, November 21, 1964, Second Vatican Council.

Excerpt from Saint Ambrose, _Exposition of the Christian Faith_, Book V, Chapter 13, Verse 168, from _Fathers of the Church, New Advent_, © 2009 Kevin Knight, http://www.newadvent.org/fathers/index.html

The seven themes of Catholic Social Teaching are taken from _Sharing Catholic Social Teaching, Challenges and Directions: Reflections of the U.S. Catholic Bishops_, USCCB, Washington, D.C. © 1998.

"We Believe, We Believe in God," © 1979, North American Liturgy Resources (NALR), 5536 NE Hassalo, Portland, OR 97213. All rights reserved. Used with permission. "Sing for Joy," © 1999, Bernadette Farrell. Published by OCP Publications, 5536 NE Hassalo, Portland, OR 97213. All rights reserved. Used with permission. "Yes, We Will Do What Jesus Says," © 1993, Daughters of Charity and Christopher Walker. Published by OCP Publications, 5536 NE Hassalo, Portland, OR 97213. All rights reserved. Used with permission. "We Celebrate with Joy," © 2000, Carey Landry. Published by OCP Publications, 5536 NE Hassalo, Portland, OR 97213. All rights reserved. Used with permission. "We Come to Ask Forgiveness," © 1986, Carey Landry and North American Liturgy Resources. All rights reserved. "Stay Awake," © 1988, 1989, 1990, Christopher Walker. Published by OCP Publications, 5536 NE Hassalo, Portland, OR 97213. All rights reserved. Used with permission. "We Remember You," © 1999, Bernadette Farrell. Published by OCP Publications, 5536 NE Hassalo, Portland, OR 97213. All rights reserved. Used with permission. "God Is Here," © 1990, Carey Landry and North American Liturgy Resources (NALR), 5536 NE Hassalo, Portland, OR 97213. All rights reserved. Used with permission. "Alleluia, We Will Listen," © 1997, Paul Inwood. Published by OCP Publications, 5536 NE Hassalo, Portland, OR 97213. All rights reserved. Used with permission. "We Believe," © 1988, Christopher Walker. Published by OCP Publications, 5536 NE Hassalo, Portland, OR 97213. All rights reserved. Used with permission. Verse text © ICEL. "A Gift from Your Children," © 1992, Nancy Bourassa and Carey Landry. All rights reserved. "Jesus, You Are Bread for Us," © 1988, Christopher Walker. Published by OCP Publications, 5536 NE Hassalo, Portland, OR 97213. All rights reserved. Used with permission. "Take the Word of God with You," text © 1991, James Harrison. Music © 1991, Christopher Walker. Text and music published by OCP Publications, 5536 NE Hassalo, Portland, OR 97213. All rights reserved. Used with permission. "We Are Yours, O Lord," © 1996, Janet Vogt. Published by OCP Publications, 5536 NE Hassalo, Portland, OR 97213. All rights reserved. Used with permission. "Alleluia, We Will Listen," © 1997, Paul Inwood. Published by OCP Publications, 5536 NE Hassalo, Portland, OR 97213. All rights reserved. Used with permission. "God Has Made Us a Family," © 1986, Carey Landry and North American Liturgy Resources (NALR), 5536 NE Hassalo, Portland, OR 97213. All rights reserved. Used with permission. "Rejoice in the Lord Always," this arrangement © 1975, North American Liturgy Resources. All rights reserved. "Sing Hosanna," © 1997, Jack Miffleton. Published by OCP Publications, 5536 NE Hassalo, Portland, OR 97213. All rights reserved. Used with permission. "Litany of Saints," © 1992, John Schiavone. Published by OCP Publications, 5536 NE Hassalo, Portland, OR 97213. All rights reserved. Used with permission. "A Circle of Love," © 1991, Felicia Sandler. Published by OCP Publications. All rights reserved. "God Made the World," © 1997, Jack Miffleton. Published by OCP Publications, 5536 NE Hassalo, Portland, OR 97213. All rights reserved. Used with permission. "This Is the Day," Text: Irregular; Based on Psalm 118:24; adapt. by Les Garrett. Text and music © 1967, Scripture in Song (a division of Integrity Music, Inc.). All rights reserved.

Printed in the United States of America.

S® is a registered trademark of William H. Sadlier, Inc.
WE BELIEVE™ is a trademark of William H. Sadlier, Inc.

William H. Sadlier, Inc.
9 Pine Street
New York, NY 10005-4700

ISBN: 978-0-8215-3052-8
3 4 5 6 7 8 9 WEBC 20 19 18 17 16

Photo Credits

Cover: Getty Images/Mitsushi Okada: *sunflower field*; Used under license from Shutterstock.com/Nagel Photography: *Cathedral of the Immaculate Conception, Albany, NY*. Interior: age fotostock/Shannon Fagan: R27; Leonov: R9. Alamy/Blend Images/Dave & Les Jacobs: 129 *bottom*; Corbis Super RF/Randy Faris: 15 *bottom*, 117 *bottom*; Heritage Image Partnership Ltd: 346; INTERFOTO Pressebildagentur: 292; Lebrecht Music and Arts Photo Library: 246; Miguel A Muñoz Pellicer: 348 *bottom*. Eakal Ali: 219, 286–287, 302 *top center*. AP Photo/Gregorio Borgia: R6; Ben Margot: 291; Alessandra Tarantino: 245 *center left*, 264–265 *top*. Art Resource, NY/Giraudon/The Solitude of Christ by Maurice Denis, © 2014 Artists Rights Society (ARS), New York, Paris: 276. Lori Berkowitz: 130. Jane Bernard: 49, 80, 88, 169 *left*, 176, 178, 179, 181, 191 *top*, 197, 232, 331. Bridgeman Images/Boltin Picture Library : 287; © Look and Learn/Private Collection/The Miracle of the Loaves and Fishes, Copping Harold (1863–1932): R11. Karen Callaway: 7, 8 *bottom right*, 17 *right*, 17 *center*, 17 *center right*, 45, 56, 61, 62, 64, 71, 72 *bottom*, 73, 75 *right*, 79 *right*, 93 *center*, 95, 97, 107 *top left*, 112, 135, 136 *bottom*, 144, 145, 146, 147, 148, 149, 152, 169 *right*, 169 *center right*, 169 *center*, 187, 188–189, 191 *bottom*, 196, 200–201, 203, 208, 210, 211, 213, 214, 215, 217 *top*, 220 *bottom*, 221, 222 *top*, 253, 267 *bottom*, 321, 322 *top right*, 322 *top left*, 322 *bottom right*, 323 *bottom right*, 323 *bottom left*, 324 *top right*, 324 *top left*, 324 *bottom right*, 332, 333. Corbis/Paul Barton: 151 *bottom right*; Jonathan Blair: 266 *bottom*, 269; Ed Bock: 114; Digital Stock: 296–297, 300–301; Randy Faris: 164; Stuart Freedman: 280 *top*; Raymond Gehman: 203 *bottom right*; Godong/ P. Deliss: 348 *top*; Danny Lehman: 180 *bottom*; LWA-Dan Tardif: 151 *bottom left*; Tom & Dee Ann McCarthy: 300; Ocean/13/Paul Burns: 347 *bottom*; Jose Luis Pelaez: 349; Pierre Perrin: 202 *top*; Michael Pole: 129 *bottom*; Tom Roberton: 150 *left*; Charles Smith: 261 *bottom*; Steve Wilkings: 25; zefa/Rob Levine: 16 *top*. Daughters of Charity Archives, Emmitsburg, Maryland: 257. Dreamstime.com/ Andy2000soft: 226–227; Thomas Dutour: 220–221; Juraj Patekar: 58–59; Phanumassu: 74–75; Volodymyr Shevchuk: 221. Eyekons/©2011 John August Swanson: 353. Neal Farris: 14, 19, 31, 43, 45 *right*, 74, 75 *left*, 79 *top left*, 93 *right*, 103, 110 *top*, 138, 139, 151 *top*, 155, 156 *center right*, 171, 183, 193, 222 *bottom*, 231, 234, 245 *right*, 252 *right*, 266 *top*, 272, 278, 296 *bottom*, 297, 304, 320, 330. Getty Images/ David Buffington: 85; C Squared Studios: 208 *top*; Joel Carillet: 351 *bottom*; Fred Derwal: R1; KidStock: R28 *top left*; Rich Legg: R28 *top right*; Dick Luria: 156 *center left*; Leon Mead: R3 *bottom*; Photodisc: 23, 107 *bottom right*, 111, 150 *right*, 208–209, 212–213, 249, 266–267, 298, 302 *top left*, 302 *top right*, 302 *center left*, 302 *center right*, 302 *bottom right*, 303 *top right*, 303 *top left*, 303 *center*, 303 *bottom left*; Stephen Simpson: 107 *bottom center*, 137 *bottom*; Stockbyte: 59 *top right*, 137 *top*, 245 *left*, 251 *bottom*; Arthur Tilley: R25; Time & Life Pictures/Steve Liss: 245 *center*, 279; Ted Wood: 219. Fotolia.com/jeremyculpdesign: 55 *inset globe*. Good Salt, Inc./Linda M. Lovett: 345; Providence Collection: 347 *top*. iStockphoto.com/Rawpixel: 55. Ken Karp: 10–11, 12, 13, 15 *top*, 17 *left*, 36–37, 38–39, 76, 82, 93 *center right*, 93 *left*, 117 *top*, 119, 122, 123, 126, 127, 143, 156 *top right*, 156 *top left*, 156 *bottom right*, 156 *bottom left*, 168, 170, 172–173, R21, 212, 259, 261 *top*, 283 *right*, 295, 301, 302 *bottom left*, 303 *bottom right*, 308, 309, 317, 323 *top left*, 344. Greg Lord: 27, 29, 72–73, 249 *top*, 324 *bottom left*. Masterfile: R31 *top*. Newscom.com/Splash News/Cesare Martucci: R14. Panos Pictures/Jan Banning: 203 *center*; Mark Henley: 267 *top*; Chris Sattlberger: 203 *top*. PhotoEdit Inc./Tony Freeman: 79 *bottom left*, 233 *center*; Richard Hutchings: 233 *bottom*; Michael Newman: 233 *top*. Reuters/Jayanta Shaw: 202 *bottom*. Chris Sheridan: 199, 248 *center*, 248 *bottom*, 254, 255. Used under license from Shutterstock.com: 104; alicedaniel: R31 *bottom*; Ase: 343; Nancy Bauer: 351 *top*; Karen Grigoryan: R17; Maxim Kabakou: R1 *bottom left*; MeiKIS: R23 *bottom*; Wuttichok Painichiwarapun: R28 *bottom right*; Pixel Embargo: R29 *bottom left*; Tatiana Popova: R13; James Steidl: R3 *top*; urfin: R28 *bottom left*; worker: R12. SuperStock: R26; Blend Images: 115 *top*; Oscar Bjarnason: R22; David Lok: 251 *top*; Roy Morsch: R19; Diane Ong: 196–197, 210–211; Photononstop: R15; Purestock/Anton Vengo: R23 *top*; Shaffer Smith: 161; Jon Smyth: 307; Universal Images Group: R12. The Crosiers/Gene Plaisted, OSC: R2; 18, 50, 113, R10, 153, R20, 185, 209, R30. The Image Works/Bob Daemmrich: 224–225. The Messenger/Liz Quirin: 260, 263. Veer/Corbis/Jose L. Pelaez: 110 *bottom*; Stockbyte: 16 *bottom*. W.P. Wittman Ltd: 44, 136 *top*, 177, 198, 237, 239, 240, 252 *left*, 322 *bottom left*, 323 *top right*.

Illustrator Credits

Series Patterned Background Design: Evan Polenghi. Bernard Adnet: 43. Burgandy Beam: 70–71. Teresa Berasi: 214–215. James Bernardin: R7, 20–23, 24, 32–33, 46–47, 68, 86, 87, 90 *top*, 93, 94, 96, 98, 99, 100–101, 108, 109, 120–121, 132–133, 134, 174, 262–263, 274, 275 *inset*, 293, 299. Linda Bild: 289–290. Lisa Blackshear: 58. Joe Boddy: 281. Janet Broxon: 247, 250–251. Gwen Connelly: 254–255. Margaret Cusack: 195. Jeanne de la Houssaye: 200–201. James Elston: 242. Florentina: 172, 179. Doreen Gay-Kassel: 184–185. Ed Gazsi: 224, 284–285, 288. Adam Gordon: 43. Annie Gusman: 176–177. Lisa Henderling: 276–277. John Hovell: 222–223. Nathan Jarvis: 53, 65, 105, 141, 181. W.B. Johnston: 32, 33, 124, 125, 150–151, 174–175, 248–249. Martin Lemelman: 278. Chris Lensch: 56–57, 138–139. Andy Levine: 69. Anthony Lewis: 107. Lori Lohstoeter: 143. Diana Magnuson: R18. Bonnie Matthews: 272–273. Deborah Melmon: 271. Judith Moffatt: 131. Amy Ning: 146–147. Marian Nixon: 19. Bob Ostrom: 29, 41, 64, 128, 205, 228, 229. Donna Perrone: 148–149. Gary Phillips: 318–319. Ceciliá Pluá: 190–191, 275. Karen Pritchett: 134–135. Jesse Reisch: 183, 186–187. Saul Rosenbaum: 63. Rich Rossi: 123. Bob Shein: 97, 98–99, 198–199, 202. Neil Slave: 38–39. Suzanne Staud: 34–35. Matt Straub: 260–261. Susan Swan: 79–83, 84, 85–89, 90 *bottom*, 155, 156–157, 158, 159, 160, 161, 162–163, 164, 165, 166, 231, 232–233, 234–235, 236, 237, 238–239, 240, 241, 242, 307, 308–309, 310–311, 312. Terry Taylor: 119. Candace Whitman: 67.

The Sadlier *We Believe* Program was drawn from the wisdom of the community. It was developed by nationally recognized experts in catechesis, curriculum, and child development. These teachers of the faith and practitioners helped us to frame every lesson to be age-appropriate and appealing. In addition, a team including respected catechetical, liturgical, pastoral, and theological experts shared their insights and inspired the development of the program.

Contributors to the inspiration and development are:

Dr. Gerard F. Baumbach
Professor Emeritus, Institute for Church Life
Director Emeritus of the Echo Program
University of Notre Dame

Carole M. Eipers, D.Min.
Vice President, Executive Director
  of Catechetics
William H. Sadlier, Inc.

Theological Consultants

His Eminence Donald Cardinal Wuerl, M.A., S.T.D.
Archbishop of Washington

Most Reverend Edward K. Braxton, Ph.D., S.T.D.
Official Theological Consultant
Bishop of Belleville

Reverend Joseph A. Komonchak, Ph.D.
Professor Emeritus of Theology and Religious Studies
The Catholic University of America

Most Reverend Richard J. Malone, Th.D.
Bishop of Buffalo

Reverend Monsignor John E. Pollard, S.T.L.
Pastor, Queen of All Saints Basilica
Chicago, IL

Scriptural Consultant

Reverend Donald Senior, CP, Ph.D., S.T.D.
Member, Pontifical Biblical Commission
President Emeritus of Catholic Theological Union
Chicago, IL

Catechetical and Liturgical Consultants

Patricia Andrews
Director of Religious Education
Our Lady of Lourdes Church,
Slidell, LA

Reverend Monsignor John F. Barry, P.A.
Pastor, American Martyrs Parish
Manhattan Beach, CA

Reverend Monsignor John M. Unger
Deputy Superintendent for Catechesis
  and Evangelization
Archdiocese of St. Louis

Thomas S. Quinlan
Director, Religious Education Office
Diocese of Joliet

Curriculum and Child Development Consultants

Brother Robert R. Bimonte, FSC
President, NCEA

Sr. Carol Cimino, SSJ, Ed.D.
Superintendent, Catholic Schools
Diocese of Buffalo

Gini Shimabukuro, Ed.D.
Professor Emeritus
Catholic Educational Leadership Program
School of Education
University of San Francisco

Catholic Social Teaching Consultants

John Carr
Director
Initiative on Catholic Social Thought and Public Life
Georgetown University

Joan Rosenhauer
Executive Vice President, U.S. Operations
Catholic Relief Services
Baltimore, MD

Inculturation Consultants

Allan Figueroa Deck, S.J., Ph.D., S.T.D.
Rector of Jesuit Community
Charles Casassa Chair of Catholic Social Values
Professor
Loyola Marymount University

Kirk P. Gaddy, Ed.D.
Middle School Team Leader/Religion Teacher
St. Francis International School
Silver Spring, MD

Reverend Nguyễn Việt Hưng
Vietnamese Catechetical Committee

Dulce M. Jiménez-Abreu
Director of Bilingual Programs
William H. Sadlier, Inc.

Mariology Consultant

Sister M. Jean Frisk, ISSM, S.T.L.
International Marian Research Institute
Dayton, OH

Media/Technology Consultants

Sister Judith Dieterle, SSL
Past President, National Association of
    Catechetical Media Professionals

Robert Methven
Vice President, Digital Publisher
William H. Sadlier, Inc.

Robert T. Carson
Media Design Director
William H. Sadlier, Inc.

Writing/Development Team

Rosemary K. Calicchio
Executive Vice President, Publisher

Blake Bergen
Director of Publications

Joanne McDonald
Editorial Director

Regina Kelly
Supervising Editor

William M. Ippolito
Director of Corporate Planning

Martin Smith
Planning and Analysis
    Project Director

Dignory Reina
Editor

Peggy O'Neill
Digital Content Manager

Contributing Writers
Christian Garcia
Kathy Hendricks
Shannon Jones
Theresa MacDonald
Gloria Shahin

Suzan Laroquette
Director of Catechetical
    Consultant Services

Judith A. Devine
National Sales Consultant

Victor Valenzuela
National Religion Consultant

Publishing Operations Team

Carole Uettwiller
Vice President of Planning and
    Technology

Vince Gallo
Senior Creative Director

Francesca O'Malley
Art/Design Director

Cheryl Golding
Production Director

Monica Reece
Senior Production Manager

Jovito Pagkalinawan
Electronic Prepress Director

Design/Image Staff
Kevin Butler, Nancy Figueiredo,
Stephen Flanagan, Lorraine Forte,
Debrah Kaiser, Cesar Llacuna,
Bob Schatz, Karen Tully

Production Staff
Monica Bernier, Robin D'Amato,
Rachel Jacobs, Carol Lin,
Vincent McDonough,
Yolanda Miley, Laura Rotondi,
Allison Stearns

We are grateful to our loyal *We Believe* users whose insights and suggestions have inspired *We Believe: Catholic Identity Edition*—the premier faith formation tool built on the six tasks of catechesis.

Contents

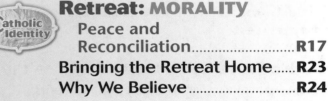

UNIT 4

WE·BELIEVE

The *We Believe* program will help us to

learn

celebrate

share

and

live our Catholic faith.

Throughout the year we will hear about many saints and holy people.

Saint Brigid

Saint Catherine of Siena

Saint Elizabeth Ann Seton

Saint Frances Cabrini

Saint Frances of Rome

Saint Francis of Assisi

Saint John Bosco

Saint Joseph

Saint Martin de Porres

Mary, Mother of God

Saint Peter

Saint Paul

Saint Philip Neri

Saint Rose of Lima

Together, let us grow as a community of faith.

Welcome!

✝ We Gather in Prayer

Leader: Welcome everyone to Grade 2 *We Believe*.
As we begin each chapter, we gather in prayer.
We pray to God together.

Let us sing the *We Believe* song!

🎵 We Believe, We Believe in God

We believe in God;
We believe, we believe in Jesus;
We believe in the Spirit
who gives us life.

We believe, we believe
in God.

When we see **We Gather** we come together as a class.

When we see **We Believe** we learn more about our Catholic faith.

Each day we learn more about God.

WE GATHER

We begin by taking a moment to pray.

✝ *Thank you, God, for all our classmates.*

Then we

think about
talk about
write about
draw about
act out

Life

at home
in our neighborhood
at school
in our parish
in our world

Talk about your life right now.

What groups do you belong to?

Why do you like to be a member of these groups?

WE BELIEVE

We learn about

- God the Father, God the Son, and God the Holy Spirit
- Jesus, the Son of God who became one of us
- the Church and its teachings.

We find out about the different ways Catholics live their faith and celebrate God's love.

is an open Bible. When we see it with a blue Scripture reference, what follows is a paraphrase of the Bible.

When we see a black reference like this (John 13:34), that passage is directly from the Bible.

Each of these signs points out something special that we are going to do.

---

means that we will make the Sign of the Cross and pray as we begin our lesson.

Key Word means it is time to review the important words we have learned in the day's lesson.

---

means we have an activity. We might

talk write act
draw
sing
work together imagine

There are all kinds of activities! We might see in any part of our day's lesson. Be on the lookout!

---

means it's time to sing! We sing songs we know, make up our own songs, and sing along with those in our *We Believe* music program.

As Catholics...

Here we discover something special about our faith. Don't forget to read it!

WE RESPOND

We can respond by

- thinking about ways our faith affects the things we say and do

- sharing our thoughts and feelings

- praying to God.

Then in our homes, neighborhood, school, parish, and world, we can say and do the things that show love for God and others.

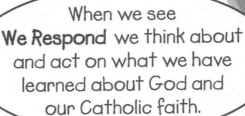

When we see **We Respond** we think about and act on what we have learned about God and our Catholic faith.

In this space, draw yourself as a *We Believe* second grader.

We are so happy you are with us!

We sharpen
our disciple skills
with each chapter's
Project Disciple pages!

Show What you Know
We "show what we know" about each chapter's content. A disciple is always learning more about his or her faith.

Picture This Pictures are a great way for us to see and show our disciple skills.

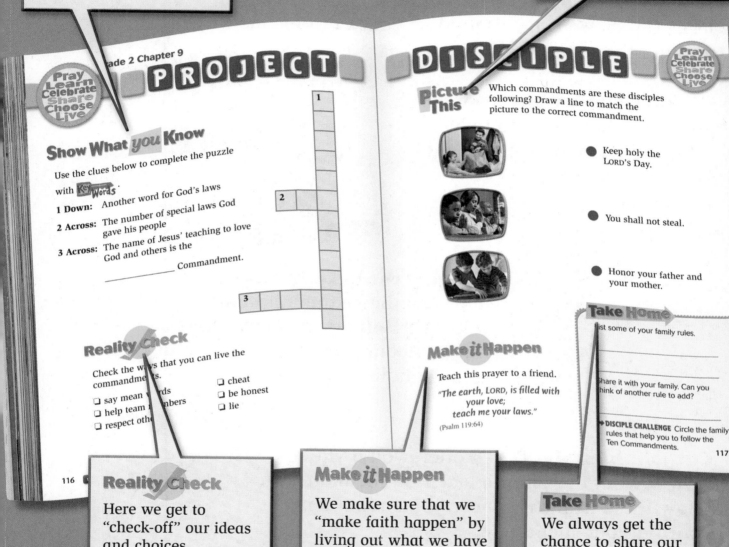

Grade 2 Chapter 9

PROJECT DISCIPLE

Show What you Know

Use the clues below to complete the puzzle with **Key Words**.

1 Down: Another word for God's laws

2 Across: The number of special laws God gave his people

3 Across: The name of Jesus' teaching to love God and others is the _____ Commandment.

Reality Check

Check the ways that you can live the commandments.

☐ say mean words
☐ help team members
☐ respect others
☐ cheat
☐ be honest
☐ lie

Picture This

Which commandments are these disciples following? Draw a line to match the picture to the correct commandment.

● Keep holy the LORD's Day.

● You shall not steal.

● Honor your father and your mother.

Make it Happen

Teach this prayer to a friend.

"The earth, LORD, is filled with your love; teach me your laws."
(Psalm 119:64)

Take Home

List some of your family rules.

Share it with your family. Can you think of another rule to add?

➤ **DISCIPLE CHALLENGE** Circle the family rules that help you to follow the Ten Commandments.

117

116

Reality Check
Here we get to "check-off" our ideas and choices.

Make it Happen
We make sure that we "make faith happen" by living out what we have learned.

Take Home
We always get the chance to share our faith "at home."

There are **LOADS of ACTIVITIES** that make us better disciples! Just look at this additional list.

What's the Word?—all about Scripture
Question Corner—take a quiz
Fast Facts—learn even more about our faith
What Would You Do?—making the right choices
Pray Today—talking and listening to God

Celebrate!—all about worshiping God
Saint Stories—finding great role models
More to Explore—getting information from the Internet and library
Now, Pass It On—invites us to witness to our faith
Don't forget to look for the **Disciple Challenge** —count how many you can do this year!

And every chapter ends with a Chapter Test!

We Believe
Catholic Identity Edition

You are on a journey to continue to grow as a disciple of Jesus Christ. You can strengthen your Catholic Identity through these new features:

Catholic Identity: Retreats

provide time for you to reflect on what it means to be a Catholic. There are four retreats in your book.

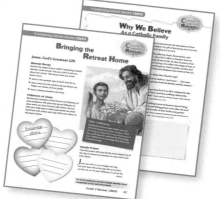

Bringing the Retreat Home helps you to share the theme and highlights of each retreat. **Why We Believe as a Catholic Family** helps you and your family to uphold and explain your Catholic faith to others.

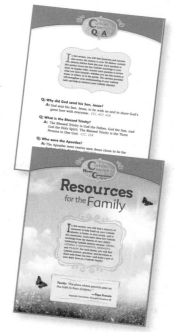

Catholic Identity: Q & A offers you a way to
review what the Church teaches. The more you know these truths the more you strengthen your Catholic Identity.

Catholic Identity: Home Companion provides
you and your family with a resource of prayers, practices, and other information to enrich your identity as a Catholic family.

Student and Family resources are available at: **religion.sadlierconnect.com**

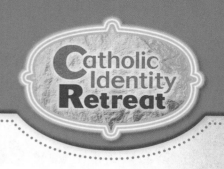

Jesus, God's Greatest Gift

Part 1 I Open My Heart

Jesus Christ is God the Father's greatest gift to us.
Look at this statue. It is called Christ the Redeemer.
It is in the country of Brazil and is 130 feet tall!
The statue reminds us of Jesus' great love for us.
Jesus' arms are open wide to everyone.

Imagine you went to visit this statue.
Write to a friend about it
on the screen below.

Jesus, God's Greatest Gift

Part 2 We Come Together for Prayer

All: (*Pray the Sign of the Cross.*)

Leader: Jesus, you are God's greatest gift to us. You forgive our sins. You love us. You show us how to love each other.

Reader 1: The name *Jesus* means "God saves." Jesus, you save us from sin. You are our Redeemer, our Savior.

All: Have mercy on us.

Reader 2: Jesus, you are Christ, the Son of God.

All: Have mercy on us.

Reader 3: Jesus, you are our True Light.

All: Have mercy on us.

Reader 4: Jesus, you are our best helper and our friend.

All: Have mercy on us.

Leader: Jesus, you . . . (*Name specific things you love about Jesus.*)

_____

_____

All: Have mercy on us. Amen.

(Adapted from a prayer by Saint Augustine of Hippo)

Jesus, God's Greatest Gift

Part 3 I Cherish God's Word

"I am the good shepherd, and I know mine and mine know me." (John 10:14)

READ the quotation from Scripture. Read slowly. Pay close attention to what you are reading.

REFLECT on what you read. Think about:

- What does a shepherd do? How is Jesus a good shepherd?

- What do you love about Jesus?

- Think about the times you have felt Jesus' love and care for you.

SHARE your thoughts and feelings with Jesus in prayer. Speak to Jesus as a friend.

CONTEMPLATE, or sit quietly and think about God's Word in the Scripture passage from the Gospel of John above.

Jesus, God's Greatest Gift

Part 4 I Value My Catholic Faith

The Redeemer and the Good Shepherd are names and images for Jesus that you have learned about. Can you think of other names and images for Jesus?

Discuss these images or names for Jesus. Choose one that you like. Write about it. Then draw that image or find a picture of it to paste or tape below.

Jesus, God's Greatest Gift

Part 5 I Celebrate Catholic Identity

Read the words inside the heart. Share how you follow Jesus. Then write your name on the line.

I am a follower
of Jesus.

_____

Make a heart out of clay. Write the name Jesus in the middle of the heart. This is a small monument to help you remember Jesus' love for you. Keep the heart in a special place at home to help you remember his love.

Jesus, God's Greatest Gift

Part 6 I Honor My Catholic Identity

All: (*Pray the Sign of the Cross.*)

Reader 1: "For God so loved the world that he gave his only Son." (John 3:16)

Leader: Let us pray: Jesus, you are the Son of God and Savior of the World. You are our friend and guide. You are the greatest sign of God's love for us. We can love others because you have shown us what it means to love each other.

Reader 2: Jesus said, "I am the way and the truth and the life." (John 14:6)

All: Jesus, we believe in you. Teach us how to love as you love. Help us to follow you every day. Amen.

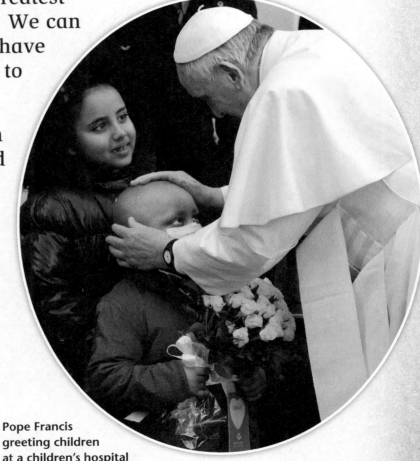

Pope Francis greeting children at a children's hospital in Rome

Catholic Identity Retreat

Bringing the Retreat Home

Jesus, God's Greatest Gift

Retreat Recap

Review the pages of your child's *Celebrating Catholic Identity: Creed* retreat. Ask your child to tell you about the retreat. Talk about what you know about Jesus:

- Jesus is the greatest sign of God's love for us.
- Jesus came into the world to be our friend, our helper, our Savior, and our guide.
- Jesus is always present in our lives.

Followers of Jesus

We become members of the Church and followers of Jesus at Baptism. We show that we are followers of Jesus when we share his love with others. Discuss with your child ways in which your family can share God's love with others each day. Write your ideas on the hearts below.

Take a Moment

During the retreat, your child explored different images or names of Jesus. Share an image of Jesus that is inspiring to you or has significance for your family. Encourage your child to share an image that he or she found inspiring.

Encourage others

Family Prayer

Pray this prayer with your family at the beginning of the day to remind one another to share God's love with others.

Jesus, be with us as we begin our day.
Let your love shine through all our actions
so that we can be your followers in all we do.
Amen.

For more resources, see the *Catholic Identity Home Companion* at the end of this book.

Why We Believe
As a Catholic Family

What if someone asks us:

- Why did God send his Son to earth?

The following resources can help us to respond:

One of the core tenets of our faith is that Jesus died and rose to save us from sin. Jesus Christ is our Redeemer, our Savior.

❧ What does Scripture say?

"For God did not send his Son into the world to condemn the world, but that the world might be saved through him." (John 3:17)

"I came so that they might have life and have it more abundantly." (John 10:10)

"Indeed, only with difficulty does one die for a just person, though perhaps for a good person one might even find courage to die. But God proves his love for us in that while we were still sinners Christ died for us." (Romans 5:7–8)

God is our Creator. God loves us. In creating us, he gave us the ability to choose how to respond to that love. That is our free will. The first human beings used their free will to turn from God. Their turning from God was the first sin. It is known as Original Sin. Original Sin weakened all of human nature.

Original Sin separated humans from God and gave us a tendency to sin. Because of Original Sin, ignorance, suffering, and death became part of our human condition. We had to be restored to our original relationship with God. And to accomplish this, God promised a Savior.

Out of his great love for us, God the Father sent his only Son, Jesus Christ, to be our Savior. Jesus Christ, the Second Person of the Blessed Trinity, is God. It is impossible to overestimate the abundance of love and generosity in this gift of becoming one of us and suffering and dying for our sins.

Through his suffering, Death, Resurrection, and Ascension, Jesus Christ offers us freedom from sin and the hope of eternal life. He also showed us how to be human beings who reflect the image of God, to be loving and forgiving. Christ's perfect sacrifice and example of love and obedience have saved us from sin.

❧ What does the Church say?

"Jesus means in Hebrew: 'God saves.' . . . The name Jesus . . . expresses both his identity and his mission." (CCC, 430)

"Everything comes from love, all is ordained for the salvation of man, God does nothing without this goal in mind." (Saint Catherine of Siena, Doctor of the Church, 1347–1380, as quoted in CCC, 313)

"There is nothing to prevent human nature's being raised up to something greater, even after sin; God permits evil in order to draw forth some greater good." (Saint Thomas Aquinas, Dominican priest and Doctor of the Church, 1225–1274, as quoted in CCC, 412)

Notes:

Jesus Christ Is With Us Always

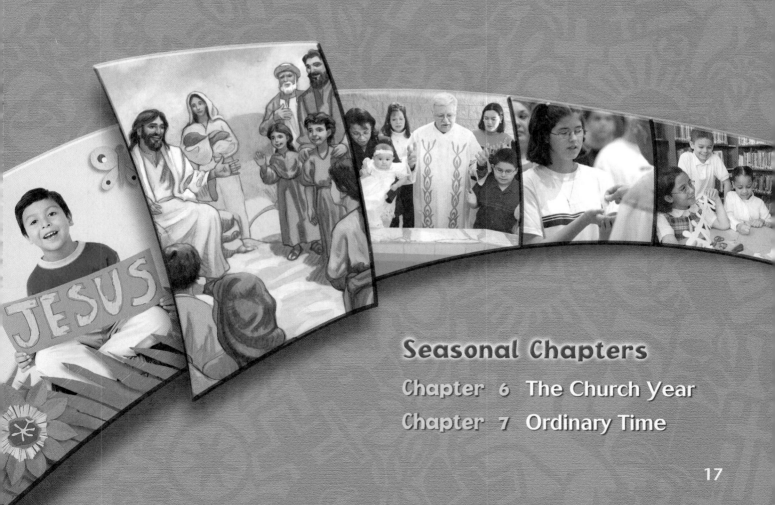

Seasonal Chapters

Pray
Learn
Celebrate
Share
Choose
Live

PROJECT DISCIPLE
DEAR FAMILY

In Unit 1 your child will grow as a disciple of Jesus by:

- learning about Jesus Christ, the Son of God, who taught us about the Father and the Holy Spirit
- appreciating that Jesus Christ gave us the Church
- celebrating with the Church community at Mass and in the sacraments
- remembering that at Baptism we received grace and that we live as children of God by what we say and do
- recognizing that the Holy Spirit strengthens those who receive Confirmation.

Saint Stories

Saint Peter was a fisherman in a small village when Jesus invited him to be his disciple. Jesus chose Peter to be the leader of the Apostles and disciples. (See Matthew 16:18–19.) After the Holy Spirit came at Pentecost, Peter traveled to many lands teaching the Good News of Jesus Christ. Eventually, Peter traveled to Rome. Roman Catholics consider Peter to be the first Bishop of Rome— therefore, the Church's first pope. We celebrate Saint Peter's feast day on June 29.

Pray Today

In this unit your child will learn that Jesus sent the Holy Spirit to his disciples to guide them. With your family, pray to the Holy Spirit often. Use the following words or make up your own.

Come, Holy Spirit, fill the hearts of your faithful.

Reality Check

"Parents have the first responsibility for the education of their children."
(Catechism of the Catholic Church, 2223)

Make it Happen

In Unit 1 your child will learn that Jesus spent a great deal of time helping his disciples become a strong, loving community. Your family is the first community your child experiences. In the coming weeks, discuss ways of strengthening your family community. Decide together on one or two specific ways you will put into action. Some suggestions are: sharing family meals (if not daily, at least once a week), showing respect for all family members, worshiping God together at Mass each week.

Take Home

Each chapter in your child's *We Believe* Grade 2 text offers a "Take Home" activity that invites your family to support your child's journey to more fully become a disciple of Christ.

Be ready for this unit's Take Home:

Chapter 1: Respecting all people

Chapter 2: Talking about Apostles and disciples

Chapter 3: Sharing ways to worship God

Chapter 4: Talking about family Baptisms

Chapter 5: Working to spread the Gospel

Jesus Is the Son of God

✝ We Gather in Prayer

Leader: Let us stand and pray.

Child 1: Glory to the Father,
All: Glory to the Father,

Child 2: and to the Son,
All: and to the Son,

Child 3: and to the Holy Spirit:
All: and to the Holy Spirit:

All: as it was in the
beginning, is now,
and will be for ever.
Amen.

God the Father sent his Son, Jesus, to be with us.

WE GATHER

✝ *God our Father, we thank you.*

Our world is filled with gifts from God. Name some. Why do you think God has given us these gifts?

WE BELIEVE

God the Father loves us very much. He gives us many gifts. He sent his Son, Jesus, to be with us. Jesus is God's greatest gift to us. Jesus is the Son of God.

Mary was a young Jewish girl. God the Father sent an angel to Mary. The angel told her that God chose her to be the Mother of his Son. Mary agreed to God's plan. The angel also told her to name the child Jesus. The name *Jesus* has a special meaning. It means "God saves."

After Jesus was born, he lived with his mother, Mary, and his foster father, Joseph. Mary and Joseph cared for Jesus, and they helped him to grow strong. We call Jesus, Mary, and Joseph the **Holy Family**.

Holy Family the family of Jesus, Mary, and Joseph

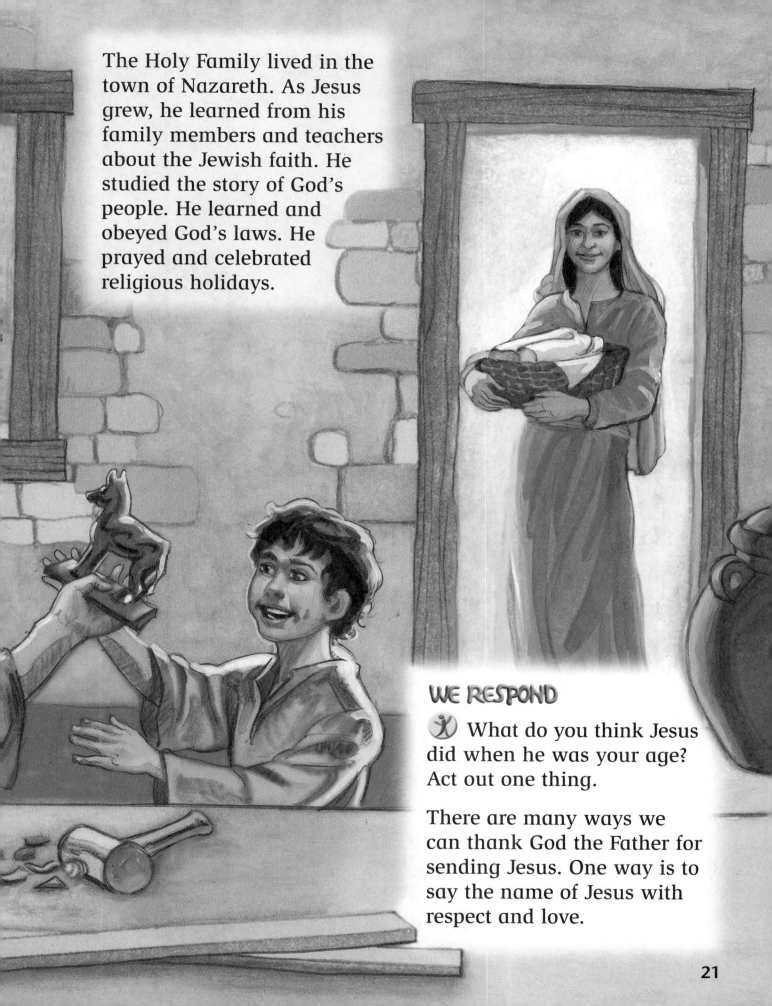

The Holy Family lived in the town of Nazareth. As Jesus grew, he learned from his family members and teachers about the Jewish faith. He studied the story of God's people. He learned and obeyed God's laws. He prayed and celebrated religious holidays.

WE RESPOND

What do you think Jesus did when he was your age? Act out one thing.

There are many ways we can thank God the Father for sending Jesus. One way is to say the name of Jesus with respect and love.

21

Jesus is human like us.

✝ *Jesus, help us as we learn more about you.*

What do we learn by listening to others?
What do we learn by watching them?

WE BELIEVE

When Jesus was about thirty years old,
he left his home town of Nazareth.
He began to teach in many towns
and villages. Jesus wanted everyone
to know that they could share in God's
great love. That was the Good News
Jesus gave to God's people.

Jesus was God's Son but he was
also human. People could see Jesus
and talk to him. They could reach
out to touch him and hear him.

Jesus told them:

- God loves all people.

- God wants all people to love
  God, to love others, and to
  love themselves.

- God is their Father.

- God should be the most
  important one in their lives.

Jesus also taught people by his
actions. He fed the hungry.
Jesus comforted those who
were sad or lonely. He
cared for the poor.

Jesus wanted people to know that God always cares for them. Jesus helped people to know that they could always pray to God his Father. Jesus taught the people a prayer that we still pray today.

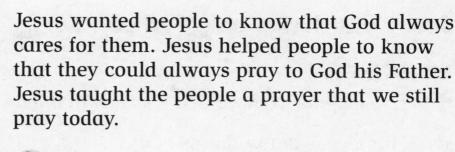 Discover the name of the prayer. Unscramble the sets of letters. Then write the name to finish the sentence.

U R O

H R A F E T

Jesus taught us

the _____.

WE RESPOND

Join together to form a circle. Now pray the Our Father together.

How did Jesus show us God's love and care?

Jesus did things only God can do.

WE GATHER

✠ *Jesus, help us to share God's love with others.*

Jesus taught us many things about God the Father. Name one you remember.

WE BELIEVE

Jesus is the Son of God. He did amazing things for people. He showed people that he was divine. **Divine** is a word we use to describe God. This means that Jesus is God and could do things only God can do.

One day Jesus visited the family of Peter, one of Jesus' closest friends.

"Jesus entered the house of Peter, and saw his mother-in-law lying in bed with a fever. He touched her hand, the fever left her, and she rose and waited on him."
(Matthew 8:14–15)

Jesus healed many other people, too. He brought people back to life. He even forgave people their sins.

♪ The words of the following song will tell you about another amazing thing Jesus did. Make up actions for the song. Sing it together.

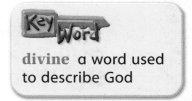

Key Word

divine a word used to describe God

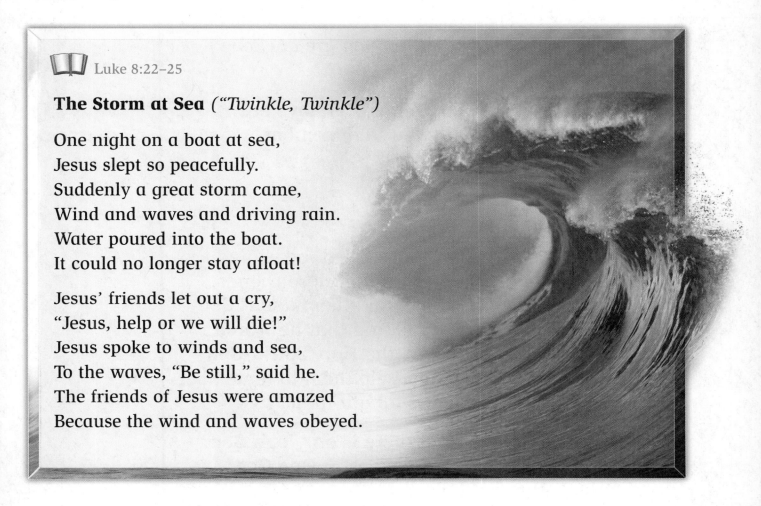

Luke 8:22–25

The Storm at Sea *("Twinkle, Twinkle")*

One night on a boat at sea,
Jesus slept so peacefully.
Suddenly a great storm came,
Wind and waves and driving rain.
Water poured into the boat.
It could no longer stay afloat!

Jesus' friends let out a cry,
"Jesus, help or we will die!"
Jesus spoke to winds and sea,
To the waves, "Be still," said he.
The friends of Jesus were amazed
Because the wind and waves obeyed.

Jesus was able to protect his friends from the storm. This was another sign that Jesus was divine.

WE RESPOND

What would you like to say to Jesus about the wonderful things he did?

Talk to Jesus now about these things. You can do this by praying in the quiet of your heart.

Jesus, the Son of God, taught us about God the Father and God the Holy Spirit.

WE GATHER

✝ *Jesus, we believe that you are the Son of God.*

Think about some things you have been taught. Who helps you to remember these things?

WE BELIEVE

On the night before Jesus died, he shared a very special meal with his close friends. They listened as Jesus told them about God the Father. Then Jesus said that he would ask his Father to send the Holy Spirit. God the Holy Spirit would help them to remember everything that Jesus taught them.

Jesus taught us that there is only one God. But there are Three Persons in One God.
The Father is God.
The Son is God.
The Holy Spirit is God.
We call the Three Persons in One God the **Blessed Trinity**.

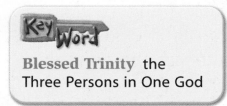

Blessed Trinity the Three Persons in One God

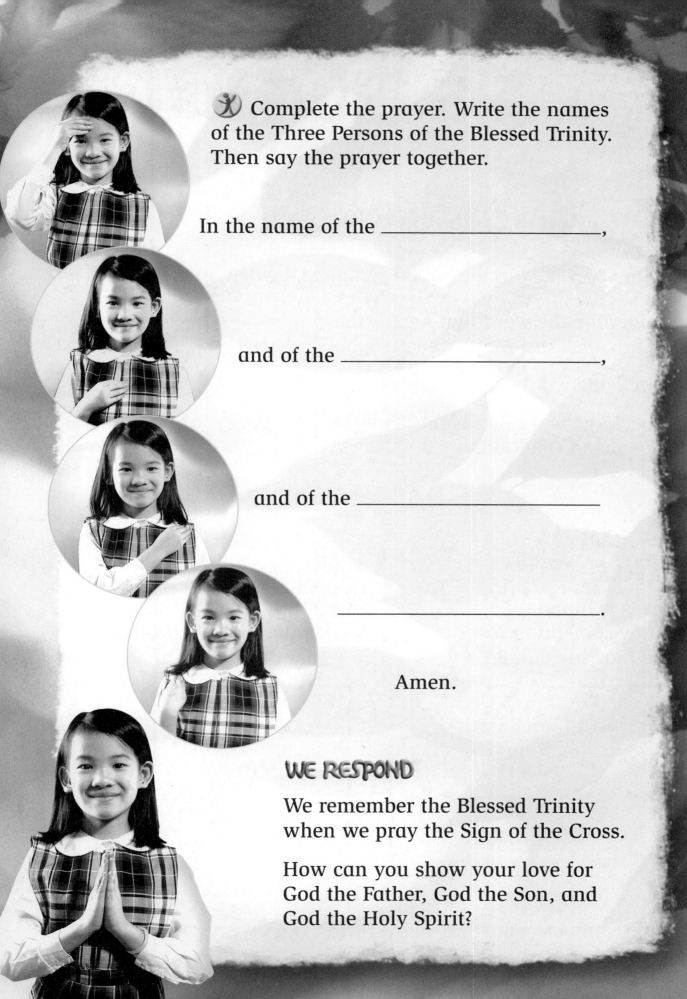

Complete the prayer. Write the names of the Three Persons of the Blessed Trinity. Then say the prayer together.

In the name of the _____,

and of the _____,

and of the _____

_____.

Amen.

WE RESPOND

We remember the Blessed Trinity when we pray the Sign of the Cross.

How can you show your love for God the Father, God the Son, and God the Holy Spirit?

27

Pray Learn Celebrate Share Choose Live

PROJECT

Show What you Know

Use the **Key Words** in the box to complete the activities below.

- Underline the word that means the family of Jesus, Mary, and Joseph.

- Circle the word used to describe God.

- Check the word that is the Three Persons in One God.

> divine
>
> Blessed Trinity
>
> Holy Family

Picture This

Jesus is human like us. Draw something Jesus did that you can do.

Jesus is divine. He did things only God can do. Draw something Jesus did that only God can do.

Pray
Learn
Celebrate
Share
Choose
Live

DISCIPLE

Pray Today

Put the parts of the prayer in order.
Number the pictures from 1 to 5.

| Amen. | and of the Son, | Spirit. | In the name of the Father, | and of the Holy |

_____   _____   _____   _____   _____

↳ **DISCIPLE CHALLENGE** Say this prayer with a friend.

Make it Happen

What is an amazing thing that Jesus did?

_____

_____

_____

Now, pass it on!

Take Home

God wants us to respect every person on earth. He wants us to respect people who are older than us. He wants us to respect people who are our age, or younger than us. He wants us to respect people who are different from us. As a family, think about some ways you can show respect to people you know.

29

CHAPTER TEST

Fill in the circle beside the correct answer.

1. The members of the Holy Family are Jesus, Mary, and _____.
   ○ Peter   ○ Joseph

2. The name _____ means "God saves."
   ○ Jesus   ○ Trinity

3. _____ told Mary God wanted her to be the Mother of his Son.
   ○ An angel   ○ Joseph

4. Because Jesus is _____, he did things only God can do.
   ○ human   ○ divine

5. The prayer we say to remember the Blessed Trinity is the _____.
   ○ Our Father   ○ Sign of the Cross

Circle the correct answer.

6. Did Jesus teach people only by things he said?   **Yes**   **No**

7. Did Jesus teach that God always cares for us?   **Yes**   **No**

8. Are there Three Persons in One God?   **Yes**   **No**

9–10. Write two things Jesus did to help people.

_____

Jesus Christ Gives Us the Church

2

✟ We Gather in Prayer

Leader: Let us take a quiet moment to listen carefully to a story about Jesus.

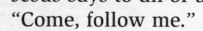 Matthew 4:18–22

One day Jesus was walking by the sea.
He saw Peter and Andrew catching fish
with a net. Jesus called them, and
asked them to come follow him.
"At once they left their nets and followed him."

(Matthew 4:20)

All: (Clap twice after each line of this response.)

Jesus says to all of us, "Come, follow me."
Come and learn how very happy you can be.
Loving God and loving others,
We are sisters now and brothers.
Jesus says to all of us,
"Come, follow me."

Jesus gathered many followers to be his disciples.

WE GATHER

✝ *Jesus, we want to follow you.*

What are some of the good or kind things that teachers do for you? What can you do to be kind to your teachers?

WE BELIEVE

Each day Jesus worked hard as a teacher. He taught people about God the Father's love for them. Jesus showed people how to love God and others. He cared for the sick and the poor. He was good and fair to everyone.

Many people were amazed at the good things Jesus did for others. They began to follow Jesus. Those who followed Jesus were called his **disciples**.

Jesus invited many people to follow him. Peter, Andrew, Mary, and Martha were some of the first disciples of Jesus.

Jesus spent a lot of time with his disciples. He cared about them very much. Jesus helped them to become a community of people who believed in him. They learned from Jesus how to love and to help one another.

From this community, Jesus chose twelve disciples to become its leaders. We call these twelve men the **Apostles**.

Jesus Christ asks you to follow him, too! He invites you to be his disciple and friend.

 Are you ready to say yes to the invitation of Jesus? Write your name on the line. Then read the sentence.

_____ is a disciple and friend of Jesus.

WE RESPOND

We are disciples of Jesus when we love God and all people. What are some ways you can show you are a disciple of Jesus?

Remember that a disciple of Jesus prays. Here is a prayer you can say each day.

Here I am, Jesus.
Thank you for inviting me
  to follow you.
I love you always! Amen.

Key Words

disciples those who follow Jesus

Apostles the twelve men chosen by Jesus to be the leaders of his disciples

33

Jesus died and rose to new life.

WE GATHER

✝ *Jesus, help us to be your disciples.*

What is a disciple?

Look at the sentences. Circle the ones that tell what a disciple of Jesus would do.

Do homework.   Tell lies.

Be kind.   Help the poor.

Be a bully.   Pray for others.

WE BELIEVE

Jesus tried to share his Good News with everyone. Some people were angry about what he taught. These people wanted to put Jesus to death.

Jesus Christ, who was both human and divine, was put to death on a cross. When he died, Jesus' human soul, united to his divine person, joined those who had died. Christ opened the gates of Heaven for those who had followed God's will.

As Catholics...

We celebrate the Resurrection of Jesus Christ at Easter and on every Sunday of the year. At every Mass we remember that Jesus died and rose to new life. Remember this at Mass this week.

 Matthew 28:1–5

Early on Sunday morning, some women disciples of Jesus went to visit the tomb where his body had been placed. What a surprise to see an angel sitting in front of the tomb! The angel said to them, "Do not be afraid!" (Matthew 28:5)

The angel told them that Jesus had risen from the dead. Jesus died and rose to new life to save us from sin. Jesus' rising from the dead is called the **Resurrection**. We celebrate Jesus' Resurrection on Easter.

WE RESPOND

🎵 Let us sing Alleluia to show our joy for all Jesus has done for us.

Sing for Joy
Sing and shout for joy, alleluia!
Sing and shout for joy, alleluia!
Sing and shout for joy, alleluia!
Alleluia! Alleluia!

Resurrection Jesus' rising from the dead

How else can you show your happiness that Jesus is risen?

35

Jesus promised to send the Holy Spirit.

WE GATHER

✝ *Alleluia, Alleluia, Alleluia.*

Do you have a close friend or relative who has moved away? How did you feel when the person first moved?

WE BELIEVE

The risen Jesus visited his disciples before he returned to his Father in Heaven. He knew that his disciples would be lonely without him. He wanted them to be close to him always. Jesus promised to send the Holy Spirit to be with his disciples and to help them.

Early one morning, the disciples were all together in one place. Mary, the mother of Jesus, and some women were there.

"And suddenly there came from the sky a noise like a strong driving wind, and it filled the entire house in which they were. Then there appeared to them tongues as of fire, which parted and came to rest on each one of them. And they were all filled with the holy Spirit . . ." (Acts of the Apostles 2:2–4)

Jesus kept his promise. God the Holy Spirit came and would be with the followers of Jesus always.

The Holy Spirit helped the disciples:

• to believe in Jesus
• to be brave in following Jesus
• to love one another
• to teach and help people as Jesus did.

We call the day the Holy Spirit came to help the disciples Pentecost. On Pentecost the Church began. The Church celebrates the Feast of Pentecost fifty days after Easter Sunday. During the whole year, we remember that the Holy Spirit is with the Church always.

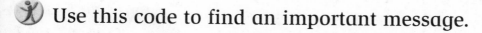

Use this code to find an important message.

A B E F G I L N O R V
1 2 3 4 5 6 7 8 9 10 11

The Holy Spirit helps us to be

___ ___ ___ ___ ___ and ___ ___ ___ ___ ___ ___ .
2 10   1 11   3   7   9 11   6   8   5

WE RESPOND

How can the Holy Spirit help you today?

Take a few quiet moments. Ask the Holy Spirit to help you follow Jesus.

The Holy Spirit helps the Church to grow.

WE GATHER

✝ *Jesus, thank you for sending the Holy Spirit.*

Think about a time you were very excited about something. You had to tell someone about it! What did you do?

WE BELIEVE

On Pentecost, the disciples of Jesus were very excited. They wanted to tell everyone about Jesus and the Gift of the Holy Spirit.

On this day Peter and some disciples spoke to a large crowd about the risen Jesus. Peter told them to be baptized and receive the Gift of the Holy Spirit.

"Those who accepted his message were baptized, and about three thousand persons were added that day." (Acts of the Apostles 2:41)

The Holy Spirit guided these first members of the Church. They met as a community and prayed together. They helped the sick and the poor. They spread the Good News that Jesus had risen.

Since the first Pentecost, the Church has continued to grow. The **Church** is all the people who are baptized in Jesus Christ and follow his teachings.

We are followers of Jesus Christ. We are members of the Church. The Holy Spirit still guides the Church every day. The Holy Spirit helps us to live as Jesus wants us to live. The Holy Spirit helps us to tell others about Jesus Christ.

Key Word

Church all the people who are baptized in Jesus Christ and follow his teachings

WE RESPOND

How exciting! You can help the Church to grow. You can do this when you do what Jesus taught.

Draw a picture to show one way you can follow Jesus.

Tell someone you know about the Good News of Jesus.

PROJECT

Show What you Know

Solve the clues below. Then find the hidden in the word search.

1. Those who follow Jesus are _____.

2. The twelve men chosen by Jesus to be the leaders of his

disciples are the _____.

3. Jesus' rising from the dead is called the _____.

```
L E S C Y T M N W D Y P
U R E R J E S L H F E E
F U L M S O H I T O N N
Y A P O S T L E S O C O
O D I I E N A M I H E I
H X C C D C A E C A B A
R E S U R R E C T I O N
N I I I R T H Q L H V R
V L D N C H I S M T Y A
```

What's the Word?

In the Bible there is a book that tells stories about the twelve men Jesus chose to be the leaders of his disciples. Guess the name of this book.

Acts of the <u>A</u> __ __ <u>o</u> __ __ <u>e</u> __

DISCIPLE

Pray
Learn
Celebrate
Share
Choose
Live

Make it Happen   Finish this disciple pledge.

I will be a disciple of Jesus.

I will be kind to _____.

I will pray for _____.

I will teach _____ how I follow Jesus.

I will show _____ how I love God and others.

What Would you do?

At recess, you see your friend Jen fall down and hurt her hand. She is crying. Draw or write what you could do as a disciple of Jesus.

Take Home

Talk as a family about ways Apostles and disciples are alike and different.

↳ **DISCIPLE CHALLENGE** Quiz your family members. Do they know how many Apostles Jesus chose?

41

CHAPTER TEST

Circle the correct answer.

1. Do we celebrate Jesus' Resurrection on Easter?   **Yes**   **No**

2. Were Peter, Andrew, Mary, and Martha the
   only disciples of Jesus?   **Yes**   **No**

3. Did the Church end on Pentecost?   **Yes**   **No**

4. Did Jesus die and rise to new life to save us?   **Yes**   **No**

Use the words in the box to complete the sentences.

5. The twelve men Jesus chose to be the leaders

   of his disciples are the _____.

| Church |
| Apostles |
| Pentecost |
| Resurrection |

6. The _____ is all the people
   who are baptized in Jesus Christ and follow
   his teachings.

7. Jesus' rising from the dead is called

   the _____.

8. The day the Holy Spirit came to help the disciples

   is _____.

9–10. Write two ways that the Holy Spirit helps the Church.

_____

We Celebrate God's Love

3

✝ We Gather in Prayer

Let us stand to pray.

Group 1

"Shout joyfully to the LORD, all you lands;
    worship the LORD with cries of gladness;
    come before him with joyful song."

Group 2

"Know that the LORD is God,
    our maker to whom we belong,
    whose people we are."

Groups 1 and 2

"Give thanks to God, bless his name;
    good indeed is the LORD,
Whose love endures forever."

Psalm 100:1–3, 4–5

We belong to the Catholic Church.

WE GATHER

✝ *Jesus, we celebrate your love.*

When people work, learn, celebrate, and share with one another in a group, they are a community.

Name some communities to which you belong. Tell what you do together in these groups.

WE BELIEVE

We belong to the Church community that is called the Catholic Church. We are **Catholics**. We become members of the Church when we are baptized. We are led and guided by the pope and bishops.

We worship and work together in communities called **parishes**. Our parish communities are led and guided by priests. They work with men and women of the parish. The whole parish serves the needs of others, especially the poor, sick, and lonely.

Some of the things that Catholics throughout the world share and celebrate are:

- the belief that Jesus is the Son of God
- the belief that Jesus suffered, died, and rose again to save us
- God's life and love
- a call to help and serve others as Jesus did.

Key Words

Catholics baptized members of the Church, led and guided by the pope and bishops

parishes communities that worship and work together

WE RESPOND

How do you think others will know that you belong to the Catholic Church?

There are many members of the Catholic Church. But each person is a **VIM**, a **V**ery **I**mportant **M**ember. The Church community needs you to pray, work, and share God's love. Talk to Jesus now about a few ways you can do this.

45

Catholics celebrate God's love by praying and worshiping.

WE GATHER

✝ *Jesus, thank you for giving us the Church.*

What does it mean to celebrate? Think about something you have celebrated. Why were you celebrating? Who was there? What did you say? What did you do?

WE BELIEVE

Jesus and his disciples often shared and celebrated their faith in God. **Faith** is a gift from God. It helps us to trust God and believe all that he tells us.

📖 Mark 11:1, 8–10

The week before Jesus' Death and Resurrection, he and his disciples were on their way to Jerusalem. Many people were gathered there to celebrate an important Jewish feast. When people heard that Jesus was coming, many went out to meet him.

Some people spread out their coats on the road. Others cut branches from nearby palm trees. They waved the branches or put them down on the road. The people called out to Jesus with the word *Hosanna*. They called,

"Hosanna!
   Blessed is he who comes in the name
      of the Lord!
Hosanna in the highest!" (Mark 11:9–10)

What did the people do to honor Jesus, the Son of God? What words did they use?

Catholics, too, gather to celebrate God's love. We **worship** God. This means we give him thanks and praise. When we gather to worship, God is with us.

We gather as a parish community each week at Mass. We celebrate all that Jesus has done for us through his life, his Death, and his Resurrection. We celebrate that Jesus is with us always. We praise God the Father, through his Son, Jesus Christ, together with the Holy Spirit. God gives us the strength to go out and share his great love.

What are prayerful actions we use to worship God at Mass?

WE RESPOND

When we worship together, we often use this word:

Alleluia

Color in these letters of the word.

What other words can you say to worship God?

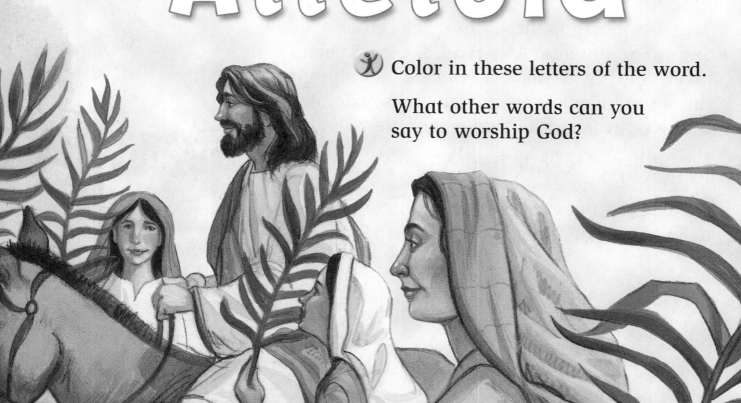

Our Church celebrates with seven special signs called sacraments.

WE GATHER

✝ *Jesus, we offer all that we say and do.*

Here are some signs of celebrations that members of communities enjoy together.

Draw lines to match each sign with a celebration.

balloon	Fourth of July parade
flag	birthday party
candy heart	Valentine's Day party

WE BELIEVE

The Church celebrates with signs, too. But the signs the Church uses are different from ordinary signs.

The special signs the Church celebrates are the Seven Sacraments. A **sacrament** is a special sign given to us by Jesus. God makes us holy through the sacraments. Jesus gave us these sacraments so that we can share in God's own life.

We gather as a Church community to celebrate these sacraments. We become stronger in faith. We grow as followers of Jesus.

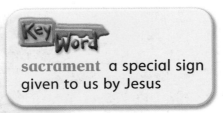

Key Word

sacrament a special sign given to us by Jesus

As Catholics...

In the Catholic Church, our parish is like our home. Millions of Catholics all around the world gather in their parish communities. In their parishes, Catholics praise and worship God. They celebrate the sacraments. They learn more about their faith. Together they do good works for the people in their communities and in the world.

What is the name of your parish?

WE RESPOND

How would you say thank you to Jesus for giving us the sacraments?
Say it now quietly and prayerfully.

Jesus is present with us in the sacraments.

WE GATHER

✝ *Jesus, we believe that you are with us always.*

👤 Think about times when a friend or a family member was away. What are some things that helped you to remember him or her?

WE BELIEVE

Through God's gift of faith, we believe Jesus is with us. Every time we celebrate the sacraments, Jesus is with us through the power of the Holy Spirit. The sacraments help us to live as friends of Jesus.

Baptism

We become children of God and members of the Church. We receive the Holy Spirit for the first time.

Confirmation

This sacrament seals us with the Gift of the Holy Spirit and strengthens us. Confirmation makes us stronger followers of Jesus.

Eucharist

This is the sacrament of the Body and Blood of Christ. We receive Jesus himself in Holy Communion.

Penance and Reconciliation

In this sacrament, God forgives our sins. We tell our sins to the priest. We are given God's forgiveness and peace.

Anointing of the Sick

This is the sacrament for those who are sick or are in danger of death. The priest prays that they may be healed in body, mind, and spirit.

Matrimony

In this sacrament, a man and a woman become husband and wife. They promise to love and be faithful to each other always.

Holy Orders

In this sacrament, a man becomes a deacon, a priest, or a bishop. He then serves the Church by leading and guiding God's people.

WE RESPOND

Which of the Seven Sacraments are you looking forward to celebrating this year?

Talk to Jesus about ways you are getting ready to celebrate this sacrament with your parish community.

PROJECT

Show What you Know

Use the code to find the Key Words.
Tell what each word means.

A	C	E	F	H	I	L	M	N	O	P	R	S	T	W
1	2	3	4	5	6	7	8	9	10	11	12	13	14	15

___ ___ ___ ___ ___   ___ ___ ___ ___ ___ ___ ___ ___ ___
 4   1   6   14 5   2   1   14 5   10 7   6   2   13

___ ___ ___ ___ ___ ___ ___   ___ ___ ___ ___ ___ ___ ___ ___
15 10 12 13 5   6   11   11 1   12 6   13 5   3   13

___ ___ ___ ___ ___ ___ ___ ___ ___
13 1   2   12 1   8   3   9   14

Celebrate! Complete this membership card.

_____
(your name)

belongs to the Catholic Church.

_____
(your name)

is a member of _____ parish.

DISCIPLE

Pray
Learn
Celebrate
Share
Choose
Live

Make it Happen   Solve this riddle.

> I am a sacrament that is celebrated by a man and a woman.
> I make them husband and wife.
> **What sacrament am I?**

Now write your own riddle about one of the sacraments. Ask a friend to guess it.

> _____
>
> _____
>
> **What sacrament am I?**

Reality Check

Which sacraments have your family members celebrated?

❏ Baptism

❏ Confirmation

❏ Eucharist

❏ Penance and Reconciliation

❏ Anointing of the Sick

❏ Matrimony

❏ Holy Orders

Take Home

Finish the sentence using words from the box.

| pray   sing   go to Mass   act like Jesus |

My favorite way to worship God is to

_____.

Ask your family members to share their favorite ways to worship God.

CHAPTER TEST

Fill in the circle beside the correct answer.

1. Jesus and his disciples _____ shared and celebrated their faith in God.
   ○ often   ○ never

2. Faith is a gift from God that helps us to trust in God and believe _____ that he tells us.
   ○ some things   ○ all

3. The Church celebrates _____ Sacraments.
   ○ Twelve   ○ Seven

4. _____ gave us the sacraments.
   ○ The disciples   ○ Jesus

5. When we celebrate the sacraments, we become _____ in faith.
   ○ stronger   ○ weaker

Circle the correct answer.

6. Are the sacraments the same as ordinary signs?   **Yes   No**

7. Do we worship God when we praise him?   **Yes   No**

8. Are parishes communities that worship and work together?   **Yes   No**

9–10. Write two things that all Catholics share and celebrate.

_____

✝ We Gather in Prayer

The word *Amen* is a prayer. When we pray this word, we are saying "Yes, we believe!" Let us respond *Amen* together after each of these prayers.

Child 1: God the Father, we believe in you.

Child 2: God the Son, we believe in you.

Child 3: God the Holy Spirit, we believe in you.

All: We are baptized. We are children of God. We live out the Good News of Jesus every day.

At Baptism we become children of God and members of the Church.

WE GATHER

✝ *Amen. Yes, we believe.*

Tell what Pedro told his aunt about Ana's celebration.

Hi, Aunt Lily! This is Pedro. We're going to have a welcome-to-our-family celebration for Ana. We're going to. . . .

WE BELIEVE

The López family is very happy! They have just welcomed a new baby into their family. The baby's name is Ana.

Soon Ana will belong to another family, the Catholic Church. In Baptism Ana will become a child of God and a member of the Church. When we were baptized, we became children of God and members of the Church. Baptism imprints on our soul a character, a permanent spiritual sign. Thus, we are only baptized once.

Ana's parents want her to be baptized. They want her to belong to Jesus and to the Church community. Everyone in Ana's family is looking forward to bringing the newest member of their family to the parish church for Baptism.

WE RESPOND

How wonderful that your family brought you to the Church to be baptized. What do you want to say to them?

Baptism is the first sacrament you receive. At your Baptism, your parish welcomed you as a new member of the Church.

Many things happened for you at your Baptism. Write your name on each line on the membership card to remember two important things. Then read the sentences.

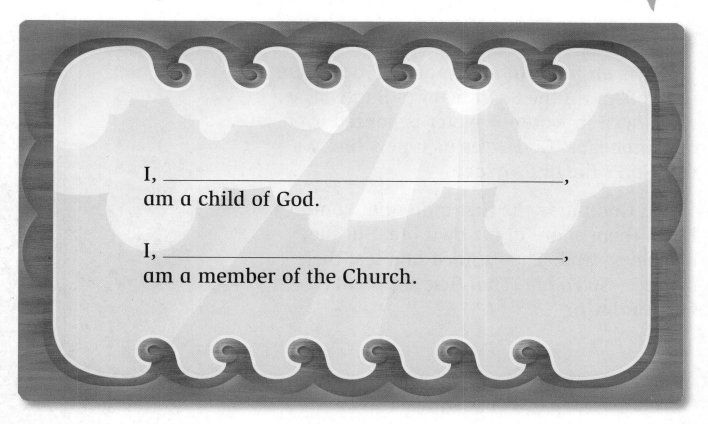

I, _____, am a child of God.

I, _____, am a member of the Church.

At Baptism we receive grace, a share in God's life.

WE GATHER

✝ *God the Father, thank you for helping us to grow.*

🧍 Finish this picture story.

Why is water important in the story?
Why is water important in our lives?

WE BELIEVE

Water is an important sign of the Sacrament of Baptism. In the Sacrament of Baptism, we are placed in water or water is poured over our foreheads. God gives us a new life. We call God's life in us **grace**.

When God made the first man and woman, he let them share in his own life. But they disobeyed God. They sinned and lost their share in God's life. That first sin is called **Original Sin**.

58

We are all born with Original Sin. Through Baptism, Original Sin and all other sins are taken away. **Baptism** is the sacrament in which we are freed from sin and given grace, a share in God's life.

WE RESPOND

Why is water a sign of our Baptism?

Close your eyes. Feel cool water pouring over you. Thank God for the gift of grace.

 Make up a tune or a special rhythm for this verse.

God's Life

When we were baptized,
we became your children.
Now we share in your life,
the life of grace.
We know you love us.
Help us grow in your love.
Thank you, God, for sharing
your life of grace with us.

Key Words

grace God's life in us

Original Sin the first man and woman disobeyed God; the first sin

Baptism the sacrament in which we are freed from sin and given grace

59

We celebrate the Sacrament of Baptism with special words and actions.

WE GATHER

✝ *God, help us grow in your love.*

Do you remember learning to pray the Sign of the Cross? Who taught you?

WE BELIEVE

This is what happened when the López family and their friends celebrated Ana's Baptism.

- Father Ramón and the parish community greeted the family.

- Father told Ana's parents and godparents that they should help Ana to keep growing in faith.

- Father traced the sign of the cross on Ana's forehead. Ana's parents and godparents did this also. This action showed that Ana now belonged to Jesus in a special way.

- Father Ramón read a story about Jesus. Father talked about the story.

- Father blessed the water in the baptismal pool.

- Father asked Ana's parents and godparents if they reject sin. He asked them if they believe in God the Father, God the Son, and God the Holy Spirit. Everyone answered, "I do" to all the questions.

- Father placed Ana in the water of the baptismal pool three times. He said the words of Baptism. It was with water and these words that Ana was baptized:

Ana, I baptize you in the name
  of the Father,
and of the Son,
and of the Holy Spirit.

Each of us was baptized with water and these same words.

WE RESPOND

Pray together these words:

O God, we thank you for our families, our godparents, and parish community. May we help each other to keep growing in your love.

Who do you think was at your Baptism? Ask your family to tell you.

We can show that we are children of God by what we say and do.

WE GATHER

✝ *Pray the Our Father together.*

Do you belong to a club or a team? What actions show others that you are a member?

WE BELIEVE

The following words and actions were also a part of the celebration of Ana's Baptism in her parish.

- Father Ramón put a white garment on Ana. He said that the white garment showed that Ana was a friend and follower of Jesus.

- Ana's godmother went to the large Easter candle by the baptismal pool. She lit a smaller candle for Ana from it. Father told Ana's parents and godparents to help keep the light of Christ burning in Ana's life.

- Father Ramón invited everyone to pray the Our Father together.

- Father blessed the family and everyone in church.

The López family will keep Ana's Baptism candle and white garment in a special place. When Ana is older, her family can use these to explain her Baptism to her.

These same words and actions were part of the celebration of your Baptism. Talk with your family. Ask them to share what they remember about your celebration.

WE RESPOND

Pray together.

Jesus, we believe that you are the Light of the World. Help us to share your light with others.

On the candle write the names of people who are helping you to become a good Catholic.

What will you do and say to share the light of Christ with others?

As Catholics...

Godmothers and godfathers are very special people. They are chosen by the parents of the child being baptized. They have a special role in this sacrament. They agree to help the parents teach the child about their Catholic faith. The godparents help the child to live as a friend of Jesus. They help the child to love God and others.

How can you say thank you to your godparents?

63

PROJECT

Show What you Know

Complete the crossword puzzle with **Key Words** .

1 Across: God's life in us

2 Down: The sacrament in which we are freed from sin and given grace

3 Across: The first sin is called

_____ Sin.

Picture This

Write what is happening in each photo from Ana's Baptism.

_____ _____ _____

_____ _____ _____

Pray
Learn
Celebrate
Share
Choose
Live

Make *it* Happen

Design a card for someone who has just been baptized.
Use words and pictures.

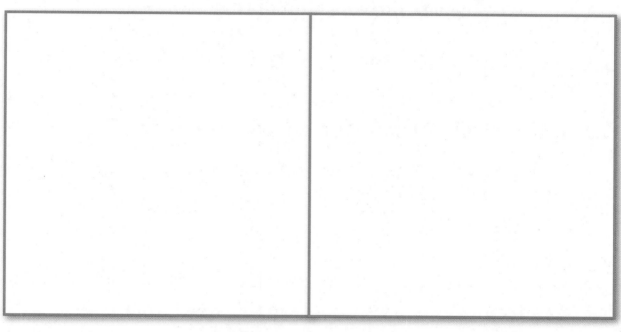

GRACE

Fast Facts

God's life in us is called grace.
Because God's grace is so
important to us, many people
name their babies Grace. More
than 92,000 baby girls have
been named Grace in the past
ten years.

(Social Security Administration, 2008)

Take Home

Interview your parents or godparents
about your Baptism. Write the
questions you will ask them.

_____

_____

_____

CHAPTER TEST

Check the sentences that tell what happens at Baptism.

1. ____ We become children of God.

2. ____ We become grandparents.

3. ____ We receive grace, a share in God's life.

4. ____ We become members of the Church.

Fill in the circle beside the correct answer.

5. When we are baptized, we are placed in _____ or it is poured on our foreheads three times.
   ○ water   ○ oil

6. When we are baptized, we are _____ Original Sin.
   ○ given   ○ freed from

7. The priest baptizes us in the name of the Father, and of the Son, and of _____.
   ○ our godparents   ○ the Holy Spirit

8. We show that we are children of God _____.
   ○ by what we say and do   ○ only by what we say

9–10. Write two reasons Baptism is a special celebration for us.

_____

We Celebrate Confirmation

✝ We Gather in Prayer

Close your eyes. Be very still.
Breathe in. Breathe out.
Try to feel God's love around you.

Join hands and form a prayer circle.
Pray the following words:

Come, Holy Spirit,
fill the hearts of your
faithful people
and kindle in us
the fire of your love.

We celebrate the Gift of the Holy Spirit in the Sacrament of Confirmation.

WE GATHER

✝ *Come, Holy Spirit.*

Do you remember what happened at Pentecost? Where were the disciples? What did they see on that day? What changed them?

 Act out the story together.

WE BELIEVE

Jesus promised to send the Holy Spirit to the Apostles and other disciples to be their helper. The Holy Spirit made them strong and brave followers of Jesus. The Holy Spirit helped the disciples to remember everything Jesus had said and done.

The Holy Spirit filled the disciples with courage and faith. They began to tell everyone about Jesus. The disciples told everyone Jesus died for us and rose to new life.

The Apostles baptized many people. They laid their hands on people so that they too might receive the Holy Spirit. They prayed for the new members of the Church. They wanted them to be strong in faith and to care for one another's needs.

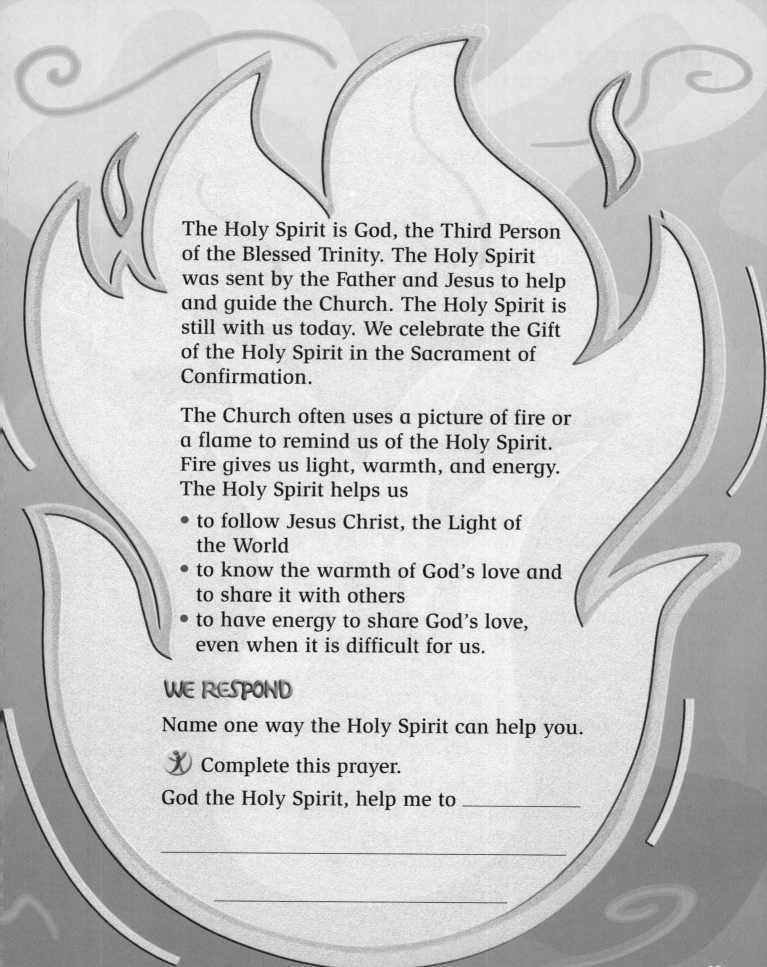

The Holy Spirit is God, the Third Person of the Blessed Trinity. The Holy Spirit was sent by the Father and Jesus to help and guide the Church. The Holy Spirit is still with us today. We celebrate the Gift of the Holy Spirit in the Sacrament of Confirmation.

The Church often uses a picture of fire or a flame to remind us of the Holy Spirit. Fire gives us light, warmth, and energy. The Holy Spirit helps us

- to follow Jesus Christ, the Light of the World
- to know the warmth of God's love and to share it with others
- to have energy to share God's love, even when it is difficult for us.

WE RESPOND

Name one way the Holy Spirit can help you.

Complete this prayer.

God the Holy Spirit, help me to _____

_____

_____

Confirmation seals us with the Gift of the Holy Spirit and strengthens us.

WE GATHER

✝ *Holy Spirit, we believe that you are with us.*

Circle the correct answers.

During gym class, you make your muscles _____.

weak   firm

Another word for firm is _____.

strong   late

What do you think *to confirm* means?

WE BELIEVE

The Sacraments of Baptism and Confirmation are like partners. Baptism makes us children of God and members of the Church. Each of us received the Holy Spirit when we were baptized. **Confirmation** is the sacrament that seals us with the Gift of the Holy Spirit and strengthens us.

In Confirmation our souls are imprinted with a character, a permanent spiritual seal. Thus, we only receive this sacrament once. The Holy Spirit helps us to be strong followers of Jesus.

Most often a bishop comes to the parish to confirm people. Sometimes the bishop appoints a priest to do the confirming. The Sacrament of Confirmation is celebrated during Mass, after the Gospel is read and explained.

Confirmation the sacrament that seals us with the Gift of the Holy Spirit and strengthens us

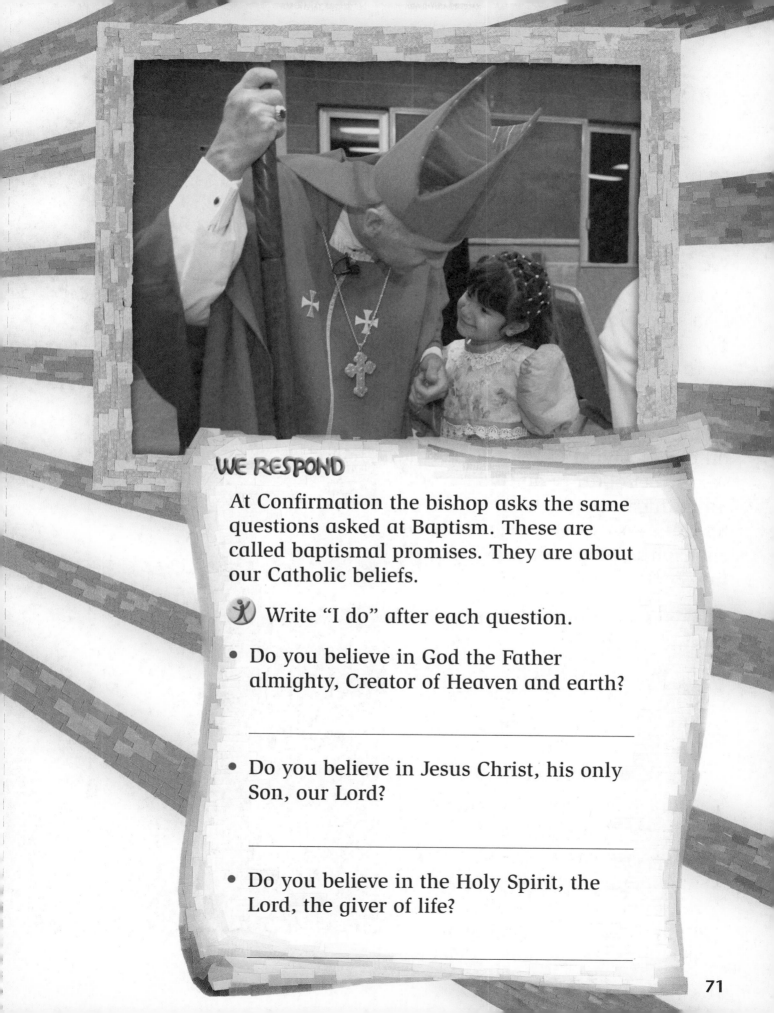

WE RESPOND

At Confirmation the bishop asks the same questions asked at Baptism. These are called baptismal promises. They are about our Catholic beliefs.

Write "I do" after each question.

- Do you believe in God the Father almighty, Creator of Heaven and earth?

_____

- Do you believe in Jesus Christ, his only Son, our Lord?

_____

- Do you believe in the Holy Spirit, the Lord, the giver of life?

_____

We celebrate the Sacrament of Confirmation with special words and actions.

WE GATHER

✝ *Holy Spirit, be our Helper and our Guide.*

What kinds of oil do we use in our homes?

WE BELIEVE

In the time of Jesus, the leaders of God's people were anointed with oil. This action showed that these leaders were set apart to do God's work. God was with the leaders in a special way.

At Confirmation we are anointed with oil called Sacred Chrism. This shows that we are set apart to do God's work. The anointing with oil shows that the Holy Spirit is with us. A person called a sponsor helps us as we get ready for Confirmation.

This is what happens during Confirmation.

- The bishop talks with the people about their faith. He calls them to live their lives in service for all. Sometimes he asks them questions, too.

- The bishop and priests who are present stretch out their hands over those receiving the sacrament. The bishop prays that the Holy Spirit will strengthen these people with special gifts.

72

• The bishop dips his right thumb in blessed oil, called Sacred Chrism. He traces a cross on each person's forehead with the Sacred Chrism. We call tracing the cross with oil the anointing with Sacred Chrism.

The bishop prays, "(Person's name), be sealed with the Gift of the Holy Spirit."

The person responds, "Amen." Then the bishop says, "Peace be with you." Those who were confirmed say, "And also with you."

As Catholics...

The week before Easter is called Holy Week. Each year during Holy Week, the bishop blesses three oils of the Church. The oils are given to all the parishes that make up the diocese. One blessed oil is called Sacred Chrism. It is used for anointing in the Sacraments of Baptism, Confirmation, and Holy Orders.

When were you anointed with Sacred Chrism?

WE RESPOND

🎵 **Make Us Strong**
("My Darling Clementine")

Holy Spirit, Holy Spirit,
Holy Spirit, make us strong,
So that we can follow Jesus
And bring God's love to everyone.

🧍 Make up actions for this song.

How can you show that the Holy Spirit is with you?

The Holy Spirit helps baptized Catholics and confirmed Catholics.

WE GATHER

✝ *Holy Spirit, stay with us always.*

Are there people in your family, school, and community who help you to learn and grow in your faith? Who are they?
How do they help you?

WE BELIEVE

The Holy Spirit helps Catholics who have been baptized and Catholics who have been confirmed to do the following things.

- Love God and others as Jesus taught.
- Worship God and celebrate the sacraments.
- Treat others with respect.
- Care for those who are poor, hungry, or sick.
- Be fair.
- Be peacemakers.
- Be happy with all that God has given them.
- Live out their faith.
- Stand up for what they believe.

Look at the pictures on these pages. For each write how the Holy Spirit is helping the people live as baptized and confirmed Catholics.

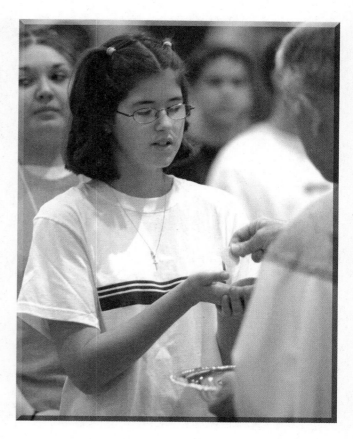

_____

_____

_____

_____

_____

WE RESPOND

Which actions listed or shown on these two pages are easy for you to do? Which are difficult?

Talk to the Holy Spirit about these ways. Ask for help with the actions that are difficult.

PROJECT

Pray Learn Celebrate Share Choose Live

Show What you Know

Use the word bank to finish this important message.

| Confirmation |
| anointing with Sacred Chrism |

The _____ _____

_____ _____ shows that the

Holy Spirit is with us at _____.

Now, pass it on!

What's the Word?

At Pentecost, the disciples were "all filled with the holy Spirit"
(Acts of the Apostles 2:4).

Remember the ways the Holy Spirit helped the disciples. Think about the ways the Holy Spirit helps us today, too.

DISCIPLE

Pray
Learn
Celebrate
Share
Choose
Live

Make it Happen

Design a poster to teach others about Confirmation. Plan it here.

What pictures will be on your poster?

What words will be on your poster?

When your poster is complete, display it in your classroom or home to share it with others.

Reality Check

Check the things the Holy Spirit helps baptized and confirmed Catholics to do.

- ❏ Be selfish
- ❏ Play fairly
- ❏ Love God and others
- ❏ Respect others
- ❏ Tell lies
- ❏ Teach others about Jesus

Take Home

The Church teaches that we should appreciate the work every person does. Talk about the kind of work the members of your family do.

↪ **DISCIPLE CHALLENGE** Talk about the ways each family member's work can spread the message of God's love.

77

CHAPTER TEST

Fill in the circle beside the correct answer.

1. The Sacrament of Confirmation seals us with the Gift of _____.

    ○ fire   ○ the Holy Spirit

2. At Confirmation the bishop or priest traces a _____ with Sacred Chrism on a person's forehead.

    ○ cross   ○ flame

3. The Church uses _____ to remind us of the Holy Spirit.

    ○ a cross   ○ fire

4. At Confirmation the _____ shows that we are set apart to do God's work.

    ○ anointing with Sacred   ○ clapping of hands
    Chrism

Check the sentences that tell what the bishop does at Confirmation.

5. ____ He pours water on a person's forehead.

6. ____ He talks with the people about their faith.

7. ____ He traces a cross on a person's forehead with Sacred Chrism.

8. ____ He prays special prayers.

9–10. Write two ways the Holy Spirit helps confirmed Catholics.

_____

Jesus said, "Follow me."

Mark 2:14

This chapter presents an overview of the Church Year.

The Church year helps us to follow Jesus.

WE GATHER

What does it mean to follow Jesus?
Name some ways you follow Jesus.

WE BELIEVE

All during the year, we gather with our parish to worship. Together we celebrate the Eucharist and the other sacraments.

The Church year is made up of special times called seasons. During the different seasons, we grow in love for Jesus. We grow as his followers.

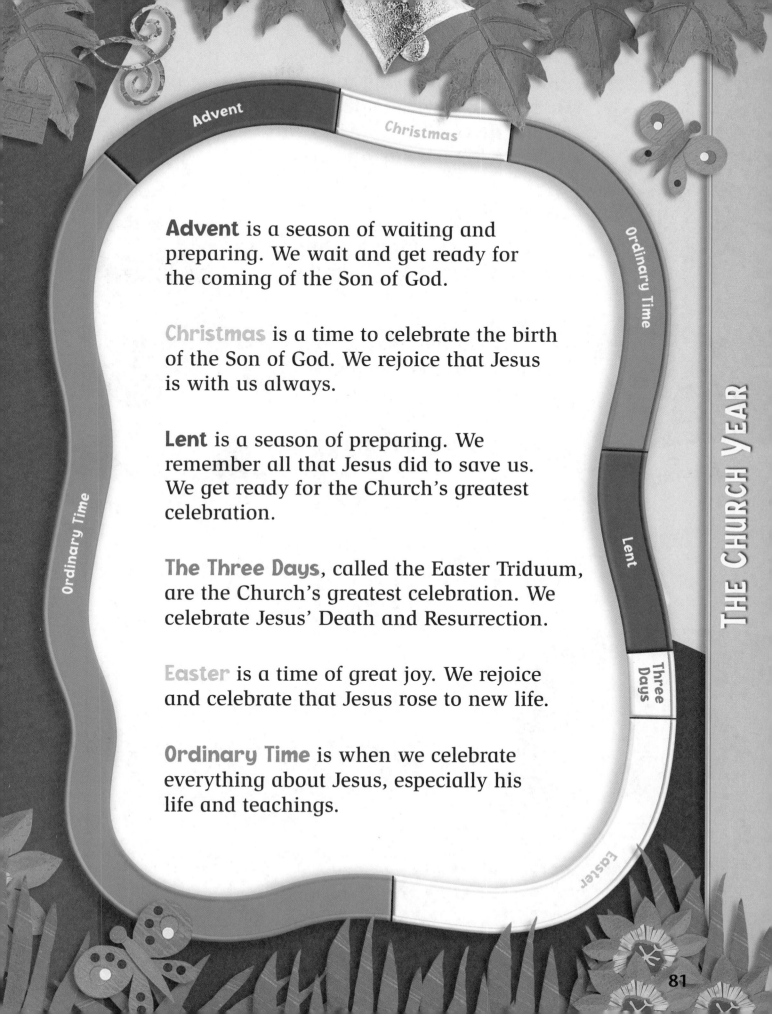

Advent

Christmas

Ordinary Time

Lent

Three Days

Easter

Ordinary Time

Advent is a season of waiting and preparing. We wait and get ready for the coming of the Son of God.

Christmas is a time to celebrate the birth of the Son of God. We rejoice that Jesus is with us always.

Lent is a season of preparing. We remember all that Jesus did to save us. We get ready for the Church's greatest celebration.

The Three Days, called the Easter Triduum, are the Church's greatest celebration. We celebrate Jesus' Death and Resurrection.

Easter is a time of great joy. We rejoice and celebrate that Jesus rose to new life.

Ordinary Time is when we celebrate everything about Jesus, especially his life and teachings.

The seasons of the Church year help us to follow Jesus. We want to grow closer to Jesus. He is God's greatest gift to us. Jesus loves us and gives us life. He is always with us. He is here, today and every day.

WE RESPOND

Each season of the Church year has a special color. Color the Church year time line to follow Jesus through the seasons. On the lines write, "Jesus, I will follow you." Then put an X on the part of the time line to show the season you are celebrating now.

Advent	Christmas	Ordinary Time	Lent	Three Days	Easter	Ordinary Time

_____

_____

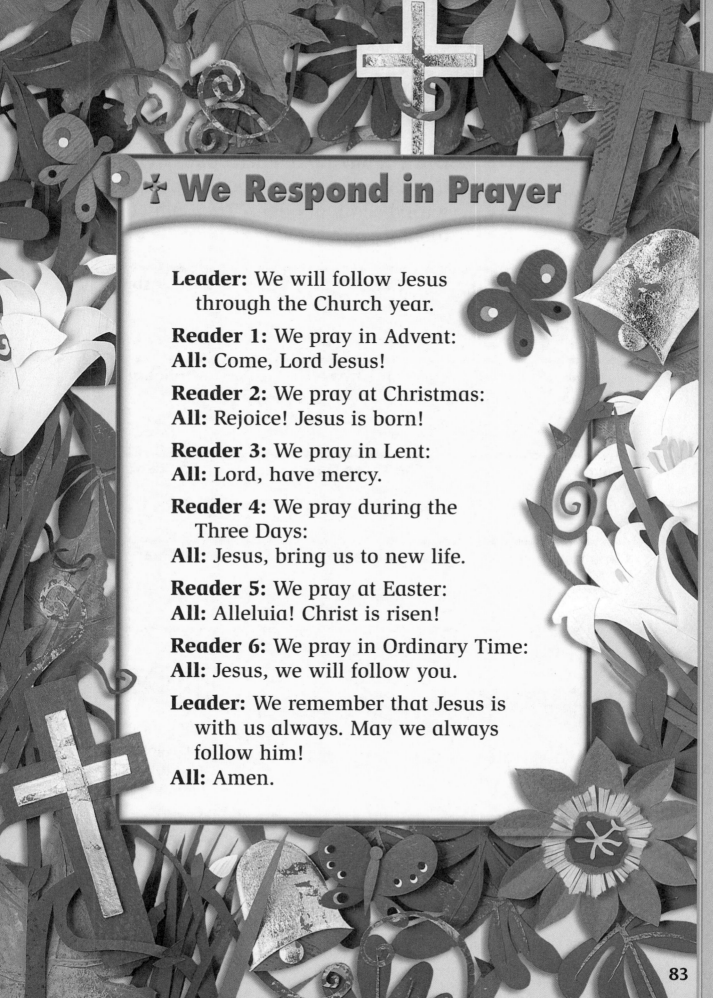

✛ We Respond in Prayer

Leader: We will follow Jesus through the Church year.

Reader 1: We pray in Advent:
All: Come, Lord Jesus!

Reader 2: We pray at Christmas:
All: Rejoice! Jesus is born!

Reader 3: We pray in Lent:
All: Lord, have mercy.

Reader 4: We pray during the Three Days:
All: Jesus, bring us to new life.

Reader 5: We pray at Easter:
All: Alleluia! Christ is risen!

Reader 6: We pray in Ordinary Time:
All: Jesus, we will follow you.

Leader: We remember that Jesus is with us always. May we always follow him!
All: Amen.

PROJECT DISCIPLE

Celebrate! Draw a picture in each space to tell about the Church season. Cover each space with a scrap of paper. Then play a memory game.

The Three Days	Lent	Easter
Advent	Christmas	Ordinary Time
Easter	The Three Days	Lent
Christmas	Advent	Ordinary Time

Reality Check

Write three ways that you can follow Jesus through the Church year.

_____

_____

_____

Take Home

Play your memory game with a family member. Take turns to find matching pairs of seasons.

↳ **DISCIPLE CHALLENGE**
When you find a matching pair, name something you do to celebrate that season.

"Every day I will bless you;
I will praise your name forever."

Psalm 145:2

SEASONAL

CHAPTER 7

This chapter helps us to understand
the season of Ordinary Time.

In Ordinary Time, we celebrate Jesus Christ and learn to follow him.

WE GATHER

What are some things that you put in order? How do you put them in order?

WE BELIEVE

What do we celebrate in Ordinary Time? We celebrate Jesus Christ! We do not remember only one event of his life. We remember and learn about his whole life, Death, and Resurrection. We celebrate Jesus Christ and everything about him!

This season is called Ordinary Time because the Church puts the Sundays in number order.

Jesus teaches the disciples to pray, "Our Father." (Matthew 6:9)

The season of Ordinary Time comes twice each year. It comes between the seasons of Christmas and Lent. Ordinary Time comes again between the Easter season and the season of Advent. The special color of Ordinary Time is green.

During Ordinary Time we:

- learn more about Jesus
- listen to his teachings read from the Bible
- learn how to follow Jesus in our everyday lives.

Look at the pictures on these pages. What does each one show you about Jesus? What does each one show about his teachings?

Jesus calls us. He says, "Let the children come to me." (Matthew 19:14)

All through the year, the most special day of the week is Sunday. Jesus rose from the dead on a Sunday.

On Sundays we gather with our parish to celebrate Mass. We listen to the Word of God and receive the Eucharist. Every Sunday, we learn more about Jesus and grow closer to him. We rest from work. We spend time with family and friends.

WE RESPOND

Draw a picture to show what your family can do on Sundays in Ordinary Time.

✝ We Respond in Prayer

Leader: In Ordinary Time, we also celebrate special days in honor of Mary, the Mother of Jesus and our mother. One of these days is the Feast of Our Lady of the Rosary on October 7.

Side 1: Hail Mary, full of grace, the Lord is with you! Blessed are you among women, and blessed is the fruit of your womb, Jesus.

Side 2: Holy Mary, Mother of God, pray for us sinners, now and at the hour of our death.

All: Amen.

Leader: Glory to the Father, and to the Son, and to the Holy Spirit:

All: As it was in the beginning, is now, and will be for ever. Amen.

🎵 Yes, We Will Do What Jesus Says

Mary said, "Do what Jesus tells you." Mary said, "Do what Jesus says." Yes, we will do what Jesus tells us, yes, we will do what Jesus says.

Question Corner

What is your favorite way to celebrate Ordinary Time? Underline it.

- learn more about Jesus
- listen to Bible stories about Jesus
- pray to Jesus everyday
- celebrate with my parish at Mass

Add another way: _____

_____

Fast Facts

Here is a sign for Mary. The M stands for Mary and for mother. There is a cross in the M. This reminds us that we honor Mary because she is the mother of Jesus.

Color this sign for Mary.

Take Home

Test your family members' knowledge of Ordinary Time. Give them this quiz.

What is the special color of Ordinary Time?

What do we celebrate in Ordinary Time?

Why is Ordinary Time called ordinary?

Fill in the circle beside the correct answer.

1. Jesus, Mary, and Joseph are called the _____.
○ Trinity   ○ Holy Family   ○ Church

2. At Baptism we receive God's life, called _____.
○ cross   ○ grace   ○ holy

3. The Church celebrates with special signs called _____.
○ grace   ○ Apostles   ○ sacraments

4. Confirmation calls us to _____.
○ live our faith   ○ be selfish   ○ be quiet

Circle the correct answer.

5. Did God the Father send his Son, Jesus, to be with us?   **Yes**   **No**

6. Are there Ten Sacraments?   **Yes**   **No**

7. Did Jesus promise to send the Holy Spirit to help his followers?   **Yes**   **No**

8. On Christmas, do we celebrate the coming of the Holy Spirit?   **Yes**   **No**

continued on next page

Write what you know about:

9. Easter Sunday

_____

_____

_____

_____

_____

10. the Blessed Trinity

_____

_____

_____

_____

_____

Jesus Calls Us to Penance and Reconciliation

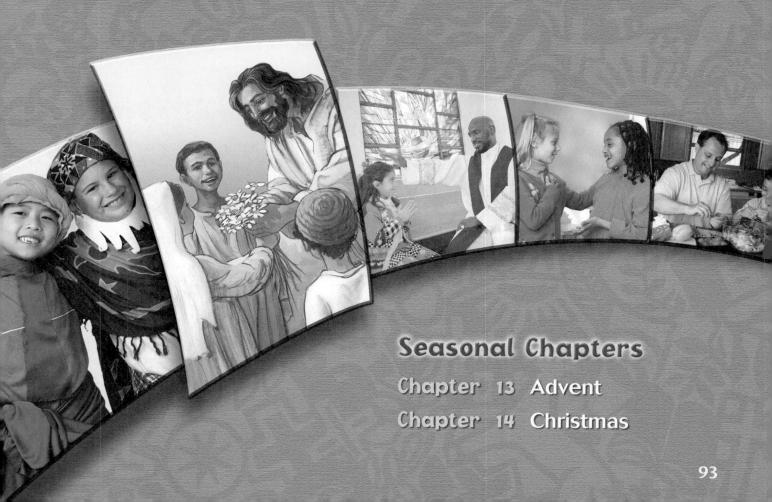

Seasonal Chapters

Pray
Learn
Celebrate
Share
Choose
Live

PROJECT DISCIPLE
DEAR FAMILY

In Unit 2 your child will grow as a disciple of Jesus by:

- understanding the importance of listening to the Word of God as found in the Old Testament and the New Testament
- learning how to live the Ten Commandments and the Great Commandment
- making choices that show love for God and others and avoiding sin
- recognizing that God always loves us and shows us mercy and asks us to forgive others
- preparing to celebrate God's forgiveness in the Sacrament of Penance and Reconciliation.

What's *the* Word?

In Chapter 11, the children hear the story of the shepherd and the lost sheep (Luke 15:4–6). Jesus told this story to show us that God will always love and forgive us. Read the story on pages 132–133 with your family. This month, make it a point to ask God for his forgiveness. And pray:

Jesus, may we never wander far from you.

Pray Today Review the list of the Ten Commandments on page 111. Then pray with your child:

God, thank you for the Ten Commandments. They help me to show love for you, for myself, and my wonderful family.

Reality Check

"The relationships within the family bring an affinity of feelings, affections and interests, arising above all from the members' respect for one another."

(Catechism of the Catholic Church, 2206)

Celebrate!

Jesus has given us a way to receive God's forgiveness. The Church celebrates this forgiveness in the Sacrament of Penance and Reconciliation. Take a moment to consider if you are receiving God's forgiveness through the sacrament on a regular basis.

Show That You Care

Point out that we can always show our love for God by forgiving one another.

Take Home

Each chapter in your child's *We Believe* Grade 2 text offers a "Take Home" activity that invites your family to support your child's journey to more fully become a disciple of Christ.

Be ready for this unit's Take Home:

Chapter 8: Discovering news about the Church

Chapter 9: Listing important family rules

Chapter 10: Discussing the qualities of a good friend

Chapter 11: Performing a scriptural puppet play

Chapter 12: Discussing the Sacrament of Penance

We Learn About God's Love

✝ We Gather in Prayer

Leader: Let us gather to listen to God's Word.

Reader: God said,
"I, the LORD, your God,
teach you what is for
your good,
and lead you on the way
you should go."
(Isaiah 48:17)

Leader: Oh God, we want to understand your Word.

All: God, help us to remember all the good things you teach us. Help us to follow your ways of love.

95

The Bible is the book of God's Word.

WE GATHER

✠ *God, we believe you are with us.*

What kind of books do you like?
What are these books about?

WE BELIEVE

God has always wanted us to
know and love him. He wants
us to tell others about him, too.

Long ago the Holy Spirit helped
certain people to write about God's
love. Different writers wrote in
different ways. Some wrote stories.
Some wrote poems. Some wrote
wise sayings. Others wrote about
interesting people and events.

These writings were put into one large
book called the Bible. The Bible has
seventy-three smaller books in it.

God the Holy Spirit guided the people
who wrote the Bible. So the **Bible** is the
book in which God's Word is written.

As Catholics...

We also call the Bible Sacred
Scripture. The word *sacred* means
"holy." The word *Scripture* comes
from a word that means "writings."

We keep the Bible in a special
place in our homes and churches.
Together make a special place in
your classroom for the Bible.

When we read the Bible, we learn:

- what God has told us about himself and his love
- what God wants us to do to live as his children.

WE RESPOND

The Bible is the most important book of all time. Why do you think this is true?

Draw a cover for the Bible. It should show that the Bible is a very special book about God.

Key Word

Bible the book in which God's Word is written

The Old Testament is the first part of the Bible.

WE GATHER

✝ *O God, thank you for speaking your Word to us.*

How do you learn about people who lived long ago?

Circle your favorite ways.

read books   watch movies

listen to stories   go to museums

check the Internet   listen to songs

WE BELIEVE

The Bible has two parts. The first part is called the **Old Testament**. In this part we learn about God's people who lived before Jesus' time on earth. We read about the many wonderful things God did for his people. We read about the ways God showed special love for them. We also learn how they showed their love for God.

In the Old Testament we learn about the lives of many people. One of the people we read about is David. When David was young, he was a shepherd. He took care of sheep near the town of Bethlehem.

God was pleased with David. God loved him very much. David was chosen by God to become king.

David showed his great love for God by praising him. David said, "Great are you, Lord GOD!" (2 Samuel 7:22)

WE RESPOND

 There are many ways to praise God. Share the words and actions you use to praise God.

The New Testament is the second part of the Bible.

WE GATHER

✝ *God, thank you for all those who tell us about your love.*

🧍 Imagine you have just heard good news. You heard that the new playground opened today. Show what you would do to share this good news.

WE BELIEVE

In Jesus' time, some people traveled from town to town to tell people what was happening.

📖 Luke 4:42–43

One morning a crowd went to see Jesus. They tried to stop him from leaving their town. But Jesus said, "To the other towns also I must proclaim the good news of the kingdom of God, because for this purpose I have been sent." (Luke 4:43)

This reading is from the second part of the Bible. The second part of the Bible is the **New Testament**. The New Testament is about Jesus Christ and his disciples. It is also about the beginning of the Church.

Four of the books in the New Testament are called the **Gospels**. They are very special. They are about Jesus' teachings and his life on earth.

The word *gospel* means "good news." Every word and action of Jesus is Good News for us. We learn the Good News of Jesus Christ in the Gospels.

- God is our Father who loves and forgives us.

- Jesus is with us always. He teaches us how to love and do good.

- The Holy Spirit helps us and guides us.

Key Words

New Testament the second part of the Bible

Gospels four of the books in the New Testament that are about Jesus' teachings and his life on earth

Make a word from each group of letters. Read the message.

S E J S U   __ __ __ __ __

H S R E S A   __ __ __ __ __ __

E H T   T H E

O D O G   __ __ __ __

E S N W   __ __ __ __

O F   O F

O D S G   __ __ __ __ ,

V E O L   __ __ __ __ .

WE RESPOND

When and where have you heard stories about Jesus? What is your favorite story about him?

Jesus wants us to listen to his teachings.

WE GATHER

✝ *Jesus, we will share your Good News.*

Imagine you are having a fire drill in school. Why does your teacher tell you to listen carefully to the directions?

WE BELIEVE

Jesus told us that it is very important to listen to his teachings. One day Jesus had been teaching for a long time. Jesus had taught people about believing in God and praying to him. Jesus ended by telling this story.

 Matthew 7:24–27

A man built his house on rock. When storms came, the wind blew. The rain beat against the house. But the house did not fall. It had been built on rock.

Jesus told the people, "Everyone who listens to these words of mine and acts on them will be like a wise man who built his house on rock." (Matthew 7:24)

When we listen to God's Word in the Bible, we hear with our ears. We remember in our minds and hearts. We show we have listened by loving God and helping others.

👤 Look at the pictures.
Write how the people are showing
that they have listened to Jesus.

_____

_____

_____

_____

WE RESPOND

What are some things you can
do to show Jesus that you have
listened to him?

_____

_____

PROJECT

Show What *you* Know

Use what you know about God's Word to complete the web.

```
                    Bible

  _____              _____
   Testament              Testament

                          Gospels
```

Pray Today

Write God a text message. Thank him for the gift of his Word. Use these words:

Word   Bible
learn   teachings
praise

To: _____ **GOD**

DISCIPLE

Pray
Learn
Celebrate
Share
Choose
Live

Make *it* Happen

Recommend your favorite Bible story to a friend. Use the form below.

I recommend _____.

It can be found in the _____ Testament.

In this story, _____

_____.

It is my favorite story because _____

_____

_____

_____

Fast Facts

More copies of the Bible have been sold than any other book ever written.

Now, pass it on!

Take Home

Ask a family member to get a copy of your local Catholic newspaper. Find out what is happening in the Catholic community.

CHAPTER TEST

Fill in the circle beside the correct answer.

1. The Bible is the book of _____ Word.
   ○ God's   ○ David's

2. The _____ Testament is the first part of the Bible.
   ○ Old   ○ New

3. The _____ Testament is the second part of the Bible.
   ○ Old   ○ New

4. We can read about Jesus' life and teachings in the _____ Testament.
   ○ Old   ○ New

5. The word _____ means "good news."
   ○ Bible   ○ gospel

Circle the correct answer.

6. Did the Holy Spirit guide the writers of the Bible?   **Yes   No**

7. Are the four Gospels about God's people before Jesus' time on earth?   **Yes   No**

8. Did all the writers of the Bible write in the same way?   **Yes   No**

9–10. Write two things we can learn when we read the Bible.

God Gives Us Laws

✝ We Gather in Prayer

Leader: Lord God, you give us life and love. Your laws help us to know how to love you and others. Show us how to follow you:

Reader 1: in our homes

Reader 2: in our parish

Reader 3: in our neighborhood

Reader 4: in our world.

All: The earth, LORD, is filled with your love; teach me your laws.

Psalm 119:64

Jesus taught us the Great Commandment.

WE GATHER

✝ *God, help us to know how to live as you want us to.*

What would you tell someone younger than you about crossing the street?

What would you tell a friend about wearing a bike helmet?

Why would you tell them these things?

WE BELIEVE

God the Father loves us very much. He cares about what happens to all of his children. God protects us by giving us laws to follow. God's laws are called **commandments**. When we follow God's laws, we will be happy.

 Matthew 22:35–39

One day Jesus was teaching. Someone asked him which commandment is the greatest. Jesus answered, "You shall love the Lord, your God, with all your heart, with all your soul, and with all your mind." Then he said, "You shall love your neighbor as yourself."

(Matthew 22:37, 39)

Jesus taught us ways to live the commandments. Jesus showed us how to love God, ourselves, and others. Jesus' teaching to love God and others is the **Great Commandment**. When we obey this commandment, we follow all of God's commandments.

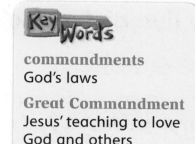

commandments
God's laws

Great Commandment
Jesus' teaching to love God and others

Look at the pictures on these two pages. For each picture write how Jesus is living the Great Commandment.

_____

_____

_____

_____

WE RESPOND

What can you do to show that you love God and others as Jesus did?

Pray quietly. Ask Jesus to help you to love God. Ask him to help you to love others as you love yourself.

The Ten Commandments help us to live as God's children.

WE GATHER

✝ *God, we will do our best today to show our love for you and others.*

What is one rule that you follow at home?

What is one rule that you follow in school?

Do you think your parents and teachers also follow rules? Why?

WE BELIEVE

Many years before Jesus was born, God gave his people special laws. These laws are called the **Ten Commandments**. They are written in the Old Testament in the Bible.

When Jesus was growing up, he learned these commandments. All during his life, he obeyed these laws. He taught his followers to obey them, too.

We show our love for God and others by obeying the Ten Commandments. The commandments help us to live as God's children. The first three commandments help us to love God. The other seven commandments help us to love ourselves and others.

Ten Commandments ten special laws God gave to his people

Here are the Ten Commandments. Remember that following them will lead you to love God and others.

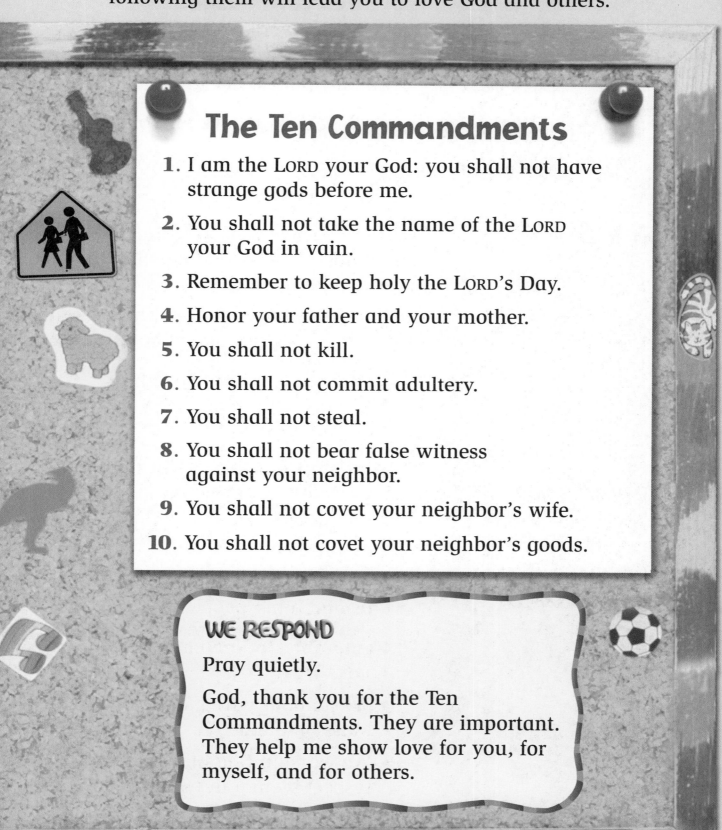

The Ten Commandments

1. I am the LORD your God: you shall not have strange gods before me.

2. You shall not take the name of the LORD your God in vain.

3. Remember to keep holy the LORD's Day.

4. Honor your father and your mother.

5. You shall not kill.

6. You shall not commit adultery.

7. You shall not steal.

8. You shall not bear false witness against your neighbor.

9. You shall not covet your neighbor's wife.

10. You shall not covet your neighbor's goods.

WE RESPOND

Pray quietly.

God, thank you for the Ten Commandments. They are important. They help me show love for you, for myself, and for others.

God wants us to show him our love and respect.

WE GATHER

✝ *God, help us to live as your children.*

How do you show love for your family and friends?

WE BELIEVE

God loves each of us very much. We must show God our love by following the first three commandments.

1. **I am the LORD your God: you shall not have strange gods before me.**

   - We believe that there is only one God.
   - We love and trust God more than anyone or anything.

2. **You shall not take the name of the LORD your God in vain.**

   - We speak God's name only with love and respect.
   - We praise God and ask him to bless us and other people.

3. **Remember to keep holy the LORD's Day.**

   - We join our parish each week for Mass on Sunday or Saturday evening.
   - We worship God and show him respect by making Sunday special.

Following these three commandments helps us to live as children of God.

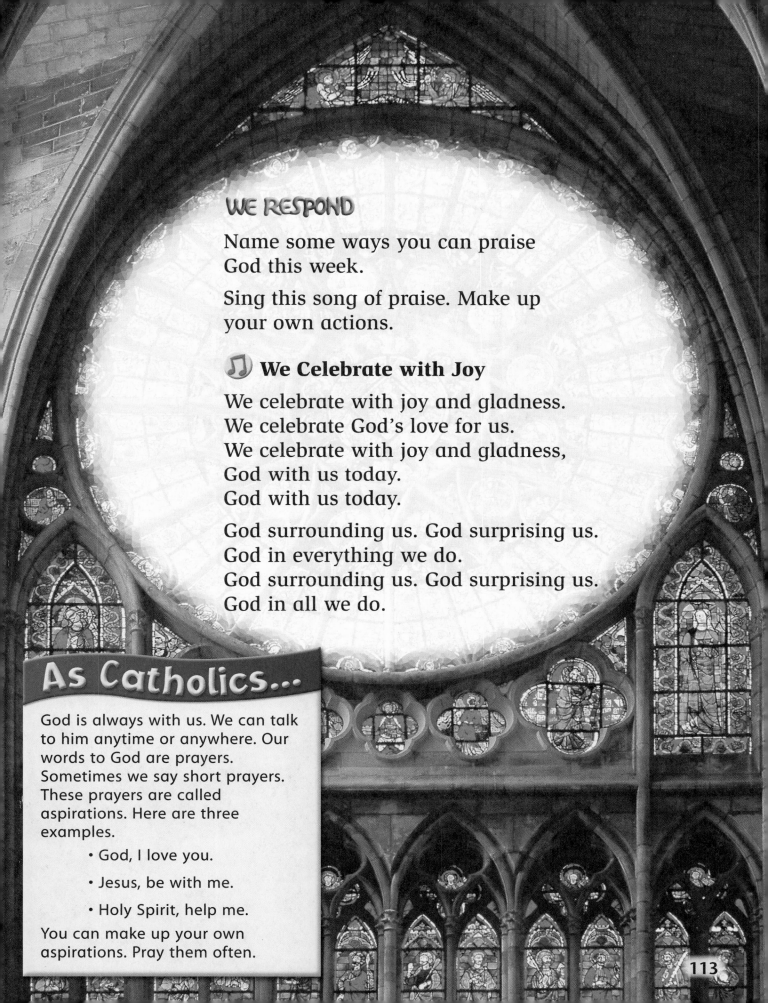

WE RESPOND

Name some ways you can praise God this week.

Sing this song of praise. Make up your own actions.

♫ We Celebrate with Joy

We celebrate with joy and gladness.
We celebrate God's love for us.
We celebrate with joy and gladness,
God with us today.
God with us today.

God surrounding us. God surprising us.
God in everything we do.
God surrounding us. God surprising us.
God in all we do.

As Catholics...

God is always with us. We can talk to him anytime or anywhere. Our words to God are prayers. Sometimes we say short prayers. These prayers are called aspirations. Here are three examples.

- God, I love you.

- Jesus, be with me.

- Holy Spirit, help me.

You can make up your own aspirations. Pray them often.

God wants us to show that we love others as we love ourselves.

WE GATHER

✞ *Holy Spirit, help us.*

How do you and your family show respect for one another? How do you and your classmates show respect for one another?

Draw a 😊 next to the ways. Add others that show respect.

_____ We do not tease one another.

_____ We take care of our things.

_____ We help one another do good things.

_____ We share our things.

_____

_____

_____

_____

WE BELIEVE

God wants us to treat one another as brothers and sisters. In the Fourth through the Tenth Commandments, we learn always to love ourselves and others.

Following the last seven commandments helps us to live as children of God.

114

Commandment	Ways to Follow the Commandment	
4 Honor your father and your mother.	• We obey our parents and all who care for us.	• We do not scream to get our way.
5 You shall not kill.	• We respect all human life.	• We do not fight or hurt anyone.
6 You shall not commit adultery.	• We respect our bodies and the bodies of others.	• We do not treat people like things. We protect everyone, especially those who cannot protect themselves.
7 You shall not steal.	• We take care of what we own. We are fair when playing. We share with those in need.	• We do not steal what other people own. We do not cheat.
8 You shall not bear false witness against your neighbor.	• We tell the truth.	• We do not say mean things about others.
9 You shall not covet your neighbor's wife.	• We show that we are happy and thankful for our family and friends.	• We do not get jealous of other people because of the friends they have.
10 You shall not covet your neighbor's goods.	• We show that we are happy and thankful for what we own.	• We do not get jealous of other people because of the things they own.

WE RESPOND

How can following the commandments help you to respect people?

PROJECT

Show What *you* Know

Use the clues below to complete the puzzle with **Key Words** .

1 Down: Another word for God's laws

2 Across: The number of special laws God gave his people

3 Across: The name of Jesus' teaching to love God and others is the

_____ Commandment.

Reality Check

Check the ways that you can live the commandments.

❏ say mean words   ❏ cheat

❏ help team members   ❏ be honest

❏ respect others   ❏ lie

DISCIPLE

Which commandments are these disciples following? Draw a line to match the picture to the correct commandment.

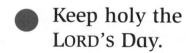 Keep holy the LORD's Day.

● You shall not steal.

● Honor your father and your mother.

List some of your family rules.

_____

_____

Share it with your family. Can you think of another rule to add?

_____

Teach this prayer to a friend.

"The earth, LORD, is filled with your love; teach me your laws."

(Psalm 119:64)

DISCIPLE CHALLENGE Circle the family rules that help you to follow the Ten Commandments.

CHAPTER TEST

Circle the correct answer.

1. Is Jesus' teaching to love God and others
the Great Commandment? **Yes** **No**

2. Should we always speak God's name with
respect? **Yes** **No**

3. Are we following the commandments
when we do not obey our parents? **Yes** **No**

4. Are we following the commandments when
we steal what other people own? **Yes** **No**

5. Do we show our love for God when we
follow the first three commandments? **Yes** **No**

Use the words in the box to complete the sentences.

6. In the Fourth through the Tenth Commandments,

we learn to always love _____ and
others.

all

respect

ourselves

children

7. When we obey the Great Commandment, we

follow _____ of God's commandments.

8. God wants us to show him our love and _____.

9. The commandments help us to live as God's _____.

10. Write one way you can follow God's commandments.

_____

We Follow God's Laws

✝ We Gather in Prayer

Leader: Let us celebrate the gift of God's laws. God gives us laws because he loves us and wants us to be happy. Listen to these words.

📖 John 15:9–10

Reader: Jesus said to his disciples, "As the Father loves me, so I also love you. Remain in my love. If you keep my commandments, you will remain in my love, just as I have kept my Father's commandments and remain in his love."

(John 15:9–10)

All: Jesus, thank you for loving us. May our love for you and others grow stronger everyday.

Jesus wants us to follow the commandments.

WE GATHER

✝ *Jesus, help us to follow your example.*

There are choices that you make each day.
Think about one choice that you made today.

WE BELIEVE

Jesus made choices all during his life on earth.
He chose to love everyone. Jesus chose to help
people even when he felt tired. He chose to spend
time with people, both the poor and the rich.
Jesus made these choices even when others did
not agree with him.

Jesus wants us to follow his example of caring for everyone. He wants us to follow the commandments. Jesus knows that it is not always easy for us to choose to love God and others. That is why he sent the Holy Spirit to help us.

WE RESPOND

Jesus chose to love everyone. He reached out to feed hungry people. He welcomed children when they ran up to meet him.

How can you follow Jesus' example?

Ask the Holy Spirit to guide you in making choices.

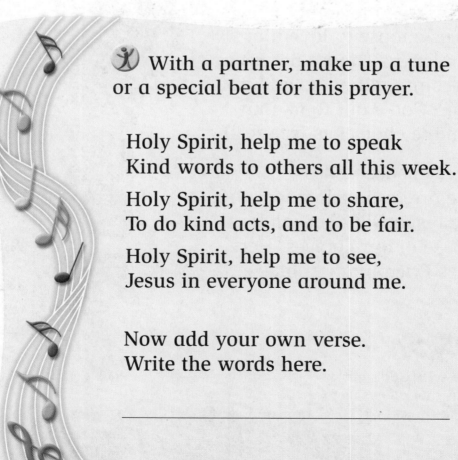

With a partner, make up a tune or a special beat for this prayer.

Holy Spirit, help me to speak
Kind words to others all this week.

Holy Spirit, help me to share,
To do kind acts, and to be fair.

Holy Spirit, help me to see,
Jesus in everyone around me.

Now add your own verse.
Write the words here.

_____

_____

God gives each person free will.

✝ *Holy Spirit, fill our hearts with love.*

What are the differences between robots and people?

 Write **P** by the sentences about people.
Write **R** by the sentences about robots.

They have feelings and can love others. _____

They can choose between right and wrong. _____

They cannot think. _____

They cannot make their own decisions. _____

WE BELIEVE

God never forces us to love and obey him. God lets us choose to love him and others. He lets us choose between following the commandments and not following them. God's gift to us that allows us to make choices is **free will**.

When we freely choose to do something, we are responsible for what we do. We are responsible for what happens because of our choices. Here are two choices Erica might make.

Key Word

free will God's gift to us that allows us to make choices

122

- Erica does her homework when her mother tells her to do it.

- Erica has a lot of homework to do. When her mother tells her to do her homework, she says, "I don't have any."

Act out what may happen because of each choice. Which was the right choice for Erica?

WE RESPOND

Stop and take time to think before you act. You can ask yourself these two questions:

- If I do this, will I show love for God, myself, and others?

- What would Jesus want me to do?

How can you know what Jesus would want you to do?

Friendship with God is hurt by sin.

WE GATHER

✝ *Holy Spirit, help us to think before we act.*

Read the following stories.

- José was setting the table. He was carrying too many dishes. He dropped his mom's favorite mug, and the mug broke.

- Nora's mom would not let her go to her friend's house. So Nora threw her mom's favorite mug on the floor. The mug broke into little pieces.

How are these stories the same? How are these stories different?

WE BELIEVE

Commit is another word for "do." **Sin** is any thought, word, or act that we freely choose to commit even though we know that it is wrong. We cannot commit sin by accident.

Some sins are very serious. These sins are **mortal sins**. People who commit these sins break their friendship with God. They do not share in God's grace, his life in them.

Venial sins are less serious than mortal sins. People who commit these sins hurt their friendship with God. But they still share in God's grace.

Key Words

sin a thought, word, or act that we freely choose to commit even though we know that it is wrong

mortal sins sins that break our friendship with God

venial sins sins that hurt our friendship with God

When we commit sin, we hurt ourselves and others, too. But it is important to always remember:

- God never stops loving us.
- God will always forgive us when we are sorry.

WE RESPOND

How can you show God that his friendship is important to you?

 Write to God about what you have learned today.

Jesus taught us about God's forgiveness.

WE GATHER

✝ *God, thank you for your love and friendship.*

How do you feel when you forgive someone?
How do you feel when someone forgives you?

WE BELIEVE

Jesus told stories to teach about God's love and forgiveness. He taught that God always loves us and is ready to forgive us. Another word for God's love and forgiveness is **mercy**.

This play comes from a story Jesus told to teach about God's mercy.

 Luke 15:11–24

All: There was a loving father who had two sons. One day the younger son asked his father for his share of the family's money.

Son: Father, I need money.
Goodbye. I've got to run.
I am going away.
I just want to have fun.

All: The young man did not always follow the Ten Commandments. He spent his money on parties and new friends.

Friends: You've lost all your money.
No more parties for you.
We don't really care
What happens to you.

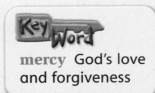

Key Word

mercy God's love and forgiveness

All: The young man began to think about the choices he had made. He remembered his father's love.

Son: I am so sorry now.
Just look what I have done!
Can my father forgive me?
I'm a very selfish son!

All: The young man was on the road home when his father saw him. The father ran to welcome him back.

Father: Son, I really missed you
And I can hardly wait
To show my love for you.
Now let's all celebrate!

"Then the celebration began."
(Luke 15:24)

The father in this story showed mercy to his son. God the Father shows each of us his mercy. He will always forgive us when we are sorry.

Act out the story of the father and the son. Then talk about the choices the father and son made.

WE RESPOND

How do you feel knowing that God is always ready to forgive you? Thank God for his great mercy.

Pray
Learn
Celebrate
Share
Choose
Live

PROJECT

Show What *you* Know

Finish the prayer using Key Words from the box.

mortal sins
venial sins

God, thank you for giving me the gift of free will. With it, I will make responsible choices. I will try not to sin.

I never want to commit _____ which break my friendship with you.

I never want to commit _____ which hurt my friendship with you.

Thank you for your mercy. Amen.

" I can push to the front of the line."

" I can wait until it's my turn."

What Would *you* do?

Ryan wants to go down the slide, but there is a long line of children in front of him. Circle the choice you think Ryan should make.

DISCIPLE

Pray
Learn
Celebrate
Share
Choose
Live

Make *it* Happen

In the chart below, write choices you can make this week to show love for God, yourself, and others.

At home, I can choose to	
At school, I can choose to	
In my neighborhood, I can choose to	
In my parish, I can choose to	

Take Home

One important decision we make in life is choosing our friends. Good friends want the best for one another. When you choose a person to be your friend, you may want to think about these questions.

- How do I act when I am with this person?
- What kind of choices do I make when I am with this person?
- Does this person want the best for me?

Survey your family members. Ask them what they look for in a friend. Together, add another question to think about when choosing friends.

_____

Now, pass it on!

CHAPTER TEST

Write *always* or *never* to complete the sentences.

1. God _____ forces us to love and obey him.

2. God _____ stops loving us.

3. God _____ forgives us if we are sorry.

Draw a line to match the sentence parts.

4. Mercy •   • is God's gift that allows us to make choices.

5. Mortal sins •   • hurt our friendship with God.

6. Venial sins •   • break our friendship with God.

7. Free will •   • is another word for God's forgiveness.

Circle the correct answer.

8. Can we commit sin by accident?   **Yes   No**

9. Does Jesus want us to follow the commandments?   **Yes   No**

10. **Write one thing we can learn in Jesus' story about the forgiving father.**

11

We Prepare for the Sacrament of Forgiveness

✛ We Gather in Prayer

Leader: Jesus is our Good Shepherd.

All: Jesus, we are the sheep of your flock.

Leader: Jesus, may we never wander far from you.

All: Jesus, Good Shepherd, hear us.

Leader: Jesus, when we have not followed your ways,

All: Forgive us and lead us back to your loving ways.

Jesus invites us to celebrate God's forgiveness.

WE GATHER

✝ *Jesus, lead us in your loving ways.*

Why do you think friends and family members forgive each other?

How do they show their forgiveness?

WE BELIEVE

When Jesus was on earth, he forgave people's sins. He showed them God's mercy. He wanted people to know that God would always love and forgive them. Jesus wanted them to understand God's forgiveness. So he told the story of the lost sheep.

 Luke 15:4–6

There was a shepherd who took care of one hundred sheep. One day one of the sheep wandered away. The shepherd left the other ninety-nine sheep. He searched for the lost one until he found it. The shepherd put the sheep on his shoulders and carried it. When he got home, he called together his friends. He said, "Rejoice with me because I have found my lost sheep." (Luke 15:6)

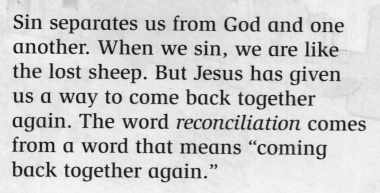

Sin separates us from God and one another. When we sin, we are like the lost sheep. But Jesus has given us a way to come back together again. The word *reconciliation* comes from a word that means "coming back together again."

Jesus has given us a way to receive God's forgiveness. The Church celebrates this forgiveness in the Sacrament of Penance and Reconciliation.

WE RESPOND

Think about Jesus' story of the lost sheep. How does it help you to know more about God's love?

Pray together.

Jesus, thank you for giving us a way to celebrate God's forgiveness and love.

133

Jesus shares God's forgiveness and peace in the Sacrament of Penance and Reconciliation.

WE GATHER

✝ *Jesus, our Good Shepherd, take care of each one of us.*

Number these sentences in order to make a reconciliation story.

_____ Teresa did not feel right because she had lied.

_____ Teresa's mom hugged her and said, "I forgive you."

_____ Teresa said, "I'm sorry, Mom. I lied to you. I won't do it again."

_____ Teresa told her mom a lie.

WE BELIEVE

God's love and forgiveness give us peace. When we sin, we are not at peace with God, ourselves, or others.

In the Gospels we read some stories about people who were not at peace with God. Jesus offered them God's love. He forgave their sins. Jesus shared God's mercy and peace with them.

Jesus gives us a way to find peace, too. He shares God's forgiveness and peace with us. In the Sacrament of **Penance and Reconciliation** we receive and celebrate God's forgiveness of our sins. We also call this sacrament the Sacrament of Penance.

Jesus gave his Apostles the power to forgive sin in his name. Today in the Sacrament of Penance, bishops and priests forgive sins in Jesus' name. They received this power to forgive sins in the Sacrament of Holy Orders.

WE RESPOND

Why does the Sacrament of Penance bring us God's peace?

Penance and Reconciliation
the sacrament in which we receive and celebrate God's forgiveness of our sins

Pray quietly. Ask Jesus to help you to be at peace with God, yourself, and others.

We examine our conscience.

✝ *Holy Spirit, send us your peace.*

It is important to stop and think about things that we do.

Think about the things that you did yesterday. Talk about some of them.

WE BELIEVE

God has given each person a **conscience**. This gift helps a person to know what is right and what is wrong.

We can prepare to celebrate the Sacrament of Penance by examining our conscience. This means we think about our thoughts, words, and actions.

The Holy Spirit helps us to remember the choices we have made. We think about whether or not we have followed God's laws. We think about the ways we have or have not followed the Ten Commandments.

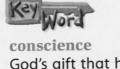

conscience
God's gift that helps us to know right from wrong

WE RESPOND

When you examine your conscience, you can ask yourself questions like these. As you read these questions, talk to God quietly about your answers.

Respect for God

- Did I always speak God's name in the right way?
- Did I pray to God?

Respect for Myself

- Did I take care of my body?
- Was I grateful for all the gifts God has given to me?

Respect for Family and Others

- Did I obey my parents and all those who care for me?
- Did I hurt someone by what I said or did?

Think about other questions you can ask yourself to examine your conscience.

Write one of them.

_____

_____

_____

We tell God we are sorry for our sins.

WE GATHER

✝ *God, please give us your mercy and peace.*

What would you say to make up with someone you hurt?

How could you show this person that you really are sorry?

WE BELIEVE

Another word for sorrow is *contrition*. We tell God we are sorry for our sins in the Sacrament of Penance. We also tell God we will try not to sin again. We do both of these things when we say a special prayer of sorrow. We call this prayer an Act of Contrition.

Here is an Act of Contrition that many people pray. Prepare for the Sacrament of Penance by learning it.

Act of Contrition

My God,
I am sorry for my sins with all my heart.
In choosing to do wrong
and failing to do good,
I have sinned against you
whom I should love above all things.
I firmly intend, with your help,
to do penance,
to sin no more,
and to avoid whatever leads me to sin.
Our Savior Jesus Christ
suffered and died for us.
In his name, my God, have mercy.

Use a different colored crayon to underline each of the following words of the prayer:

- words that tell God we are sorry

- words that promise to try not to sin again

- words that ask God to forgive us in Jesus' name.

WE RESPOND

How can you show God you are truly sorry?

Pray together the Act of Contrition on this page.

PROJECT

Pray
Learn
Celebrate
Share
Choose
Live

Show What *you* Know

Use the color code to color the  .

 green
God's gift that helps us to know right from wrong

 purple
the sacrament in which we receive and celebrate God's forgiveness of our sins

conscience

Penance and

Reconciliation

☀Celebrate!

All of us are in need of God's forgiveness. The Church encourages us to celebrate God's forgiveness in the Sacrament of Penance. If we sin in a way that breaks our friendship with God, we must tell these mortal sins to the priest. We should also tell any venial sins. They hurt our friendship with God and with one another. In the Sacrament of Penance we receive forgiveness and are at peace with God and with one another.

DISCIPLE

Pray
Learn
Celebrate
Share
Choose
Live

Make *it* Happen

With a classmate, write a skit about forgiveness. Your skit must have a beginning, a middle, and an end. Plan it out in the space below.

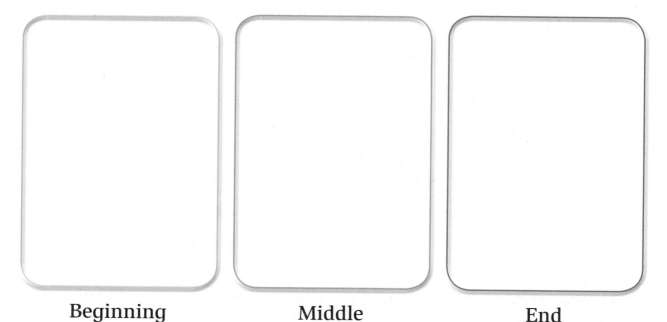

| Beginning | Middle | End |

Practice your skit together, and then act it out for your class.

Take Home

On a separate piece of paper, draw a picture of the shepherd and the lost sheep. Cut each one out. Use craft sticks to make your pictures into puppets. Perform a puppet play of the story of the lost sheep for your family.

↳ **DISCIPLE CHALLENGE** How are we like the lost sheep? How is God like the shepherd? Tell your family.

CHAPTER TEST

Fill in the circle beside the correct answer.

1. Our _____ helps us to know right from wrong.
   ○ conscience   ○ contrition

2. Penance and Reconciliation is a sacrament of _____.
   ○ forgiveness   ○ forgetting

3. We are not at peace with God, ourselves, and others when we _____.
   ○ love   ○ sin

4. A word that means "coming back together again" is _____.
   ○ reconciliation   ○ conscience

5. When we think about our thoughts, words, and actions, we examine our _____.
   ○ contrition   ○ conscience

6. _____ is another word for sorrow.
   ○ Contrition   ○ Reconciliation

7–8. Write two ways to prepare for the Sacrament of Penance.

_____

9–10. Write two things we tell God in the Act of Contrition.

_____

We Celebrate the Sacrament of Forgiveness

✟ We Gather in Prayer

🎵 We Come to Ask Forgiveness

We come to ask your forgiveness, O Lord,
and we seek forgiveness from each other.
Sometimes we build up walls instead
    of bridges to peace,
and we ask your forgiveness,
    O Lord.

For the times when we've been
    rude and selfish,
for the times when we have
    been unkind;
and for the times we refused
    to help our friends in need,
we ask your forgiveness,
    O Lord.

We ask for God's forgiveness in the Sacrament of Penance.

WE GATHER

✝ *God, we want to celebrate your forgiveness.*

Think about TV shows or movies you have watched in the past few weeks. Tell about those that were stories of forgiveness.

WE BELIEVE

We ask God for forgiveness in the Sacrament of Penance. When we celebrate the Sacrament of Penance, we think about the ways we have shown or not shown love for God and for others. This is an examination of conscience. We are sorry for our sins and promise not to sin again. This is **contrition**. If we are sorry because we love God it is perfect contrition. If we are sorry for other reasons it is imperfect contrition.

We tell our sins to the priest. This is called **confession**.

The priest tells us to say a prayer or to do a kind act to make up for our sins. This is called **a penance**.

contrition being sorry for our sins and promising not to sin again

confession telling our sins to the priest in the Sacrament of Penance

a penance a prayer or a kind act we do to make up for our sins

absolution God's forgiveness of our sins by the priest in the Sacrament of Penance

We say an Act of Contrition to tell God we are sorry. We promise not to sin again. The priest acting in the name of Jesus forgives our sins. This is called **absolution**. The word *absolution* comes from a word that means "washing away."

These steps are always part of the Sacrament of Penance. When we celebrate the Sacrament of Penance, we meet with the priest. He acts in the name of Jesus. We may sit and face the priest or kneel behind a screen.

WE RESPOND

When you celebrate this sacrament, you will receive a penance. Sometimes the priest will tell you to say a prayer. Sometimes he will tell you to do a kind act.

What are you telling God when you do the penance the priest gives you?

We celebrate God's forgiveness in the Sacrament of Penance.

WE GATHER

 God, we trust in your love and forgiveness.

This picture shows Lucy getting ready to celebrate the Sacrament of Penance. She is examining her conscience.

Write a question she can ask herself.

_____

_____

WE BELIEVE

This is what happened when Lucy went to Father Rob to celebrate the Sacrament of Penance.

- Father Rob welcomed Lucy, and they both made the Sign of the Cross.

- Lucy listened as Father Rob read a story from the Bible. The story was about God's forgiveness.

- Lucy confessed her sins to Father Rob.

- Father Rob and Lucy talked about what she could do to make right choices. Then Father gave Lucy a penance. Lucy will do her penance after the celebration of the sacrament.

- Lucy prayed an Act of Contrition.
- Lucy received absolution, or forgiveness, from her sins. Father Rob stretched out his right hand over Lucy's head. He said the following words to Lucy.

"God, the Father of mercies,
through the death and resurrection
    of his Son
has reconciled the world to himself
and sent the Holy Spirit among us
for the forgiveness of sins;
through the ministry of the Church
may God give you pardon and peace,
and I absolve you from your sins
in the name of the Father,
    and of the Son, †
and of the Holy Spirit."

Lucy answered, "Amen."

- Then Father Rob and Lucy praised and thanked God for his love and forgiveness. Father told Lucy, "Go in peace."

We can celebrate the Sacrament of Penance as Lucy did. God is always willing to give us his mercy and peace when we are sorry.

WE RESPOND

How do you think celebrating the Sacrament of Penance will help you?

As Catholics...

The parish priest is always willing to help us. He listens to us and helps us to follow Jesus. We tell the priest our sins in the Sacrament of Penance. The priest cannot tell anyone the sins we confess.

Who are the priests who will celebrate Penance with you?

We celebrate the Sacrament of Penance with our parish community.

WE GATHER

✝ *God, we celebrate your forgiveness.*

You gather with your parish community at Mass on Sunday. When are other times your parish community gathers?

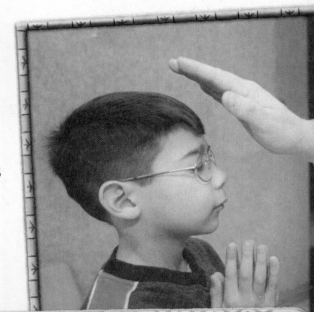

WE BELIEVE

Our parish community sometimes gathers to celebrate the Sacrament of Penance together. This helps us to see that all of us need forgiveness.

This is what happens during that celebration.

- The parish community sings a song. Then we are welcomed by the priest.

- We listen to readings from the Bible. These readings are about God's love and forgiveness.

- The priest talks to us about the readings.

- We listen to questions that are part of an examination of conscience.

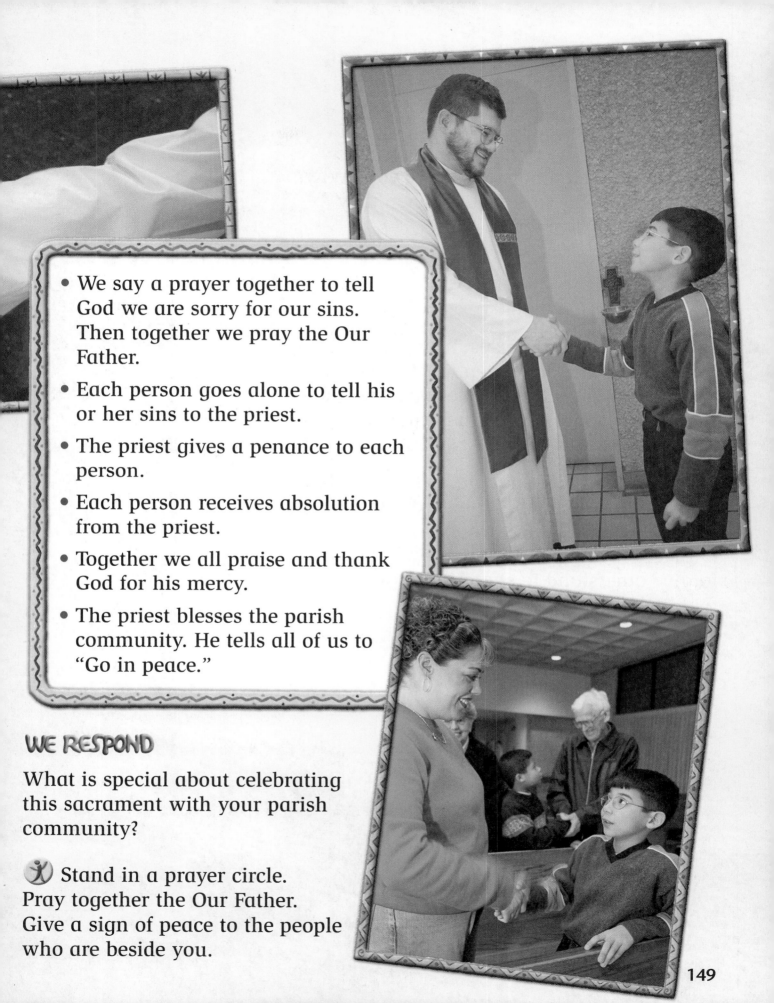

- We say a prayer together to tell God we are sorry for our sins. Then together we pray the Our Father.

- Each person goes alone to tell his or her sins to the priest.

- The priest gives a penance to each person.

- Each person receives absolution from the priest.

- Together we all praise and thank God for his mercy.

- The priest blesses the parish community. He tells all of us to "Go in peace."

WE RESPOND

What is special about celebrating this sacrament with your parish community?

Stand in a prayer circle. Pray together the Our Father. Give a sign of peace to the people who are beside you.

Jesus wants us to forgive others.

WE GATHER

✝ *Jesus, thank you for your gift of peace.*

Do you ever ask others to forgive you? Why? What do you say to someone when they ask you to forgive them?

WE BELIEVE

 Matthew 18:21–23

One day Peter asked Jesus, "Lord, if my brother sins against me, how often must I forgive him? As many as seven times?" Jesus answered, "I say to you, not seven times but seventy-seven times." (Matthew 18:21, 22)

In this story, Jesus is telling us that we should always forgive others. When we celebrate the Sacrament of Penance, we receive God's forgiveness and peace. Jesus wants us to forgive others and to share God's gift of peace with them.

Jesus wants us to be peacemakers

- wherever we are
- whenever we can
- in whatever we do.

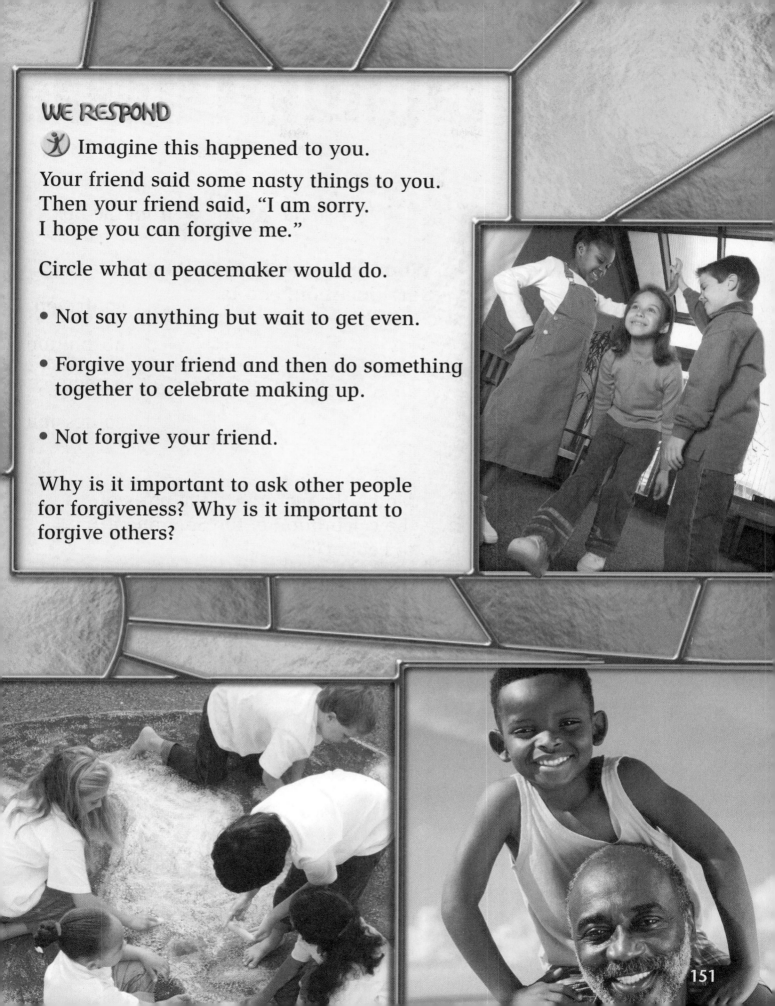

WE RESPOND

Imagine this happened to you.

Your friend said some nasty things to you.
Then your friend said, "I am sorry.
I hope you can forgive me."

Circle what a peacemaker would do.

- Not say anything but wait to get even.

- Forgive your friend and then do something together to celebrate making up.

- Not forgive your friend.

Why is it important to ask other people for forgiveness? Why is it important to forgive others?

PROJECT

Show What *you* Know

Use the Key Words from the box.

What I do in the Sacrament of Penance:

_____

_____

_____

What the priest does in the Sacrament of Penance:

_____

_____

contrition

absolution

a penance

confession

Celebrate!

Match the pictures to the parts of the celebration of the Sacrament of Penance.

● Lucy listens as Father Rob reads a story about God's forgiveness from the Bible.

● Lucy receives absolution, or forgiveness, for her sins.

● Lucy examines her conscience to prepare for the Sacrament of Penance.

DISCIPLE

Pray
Learn
Celebrate
Share
Choose
Live

Saint Stories

Saint Francis of Assisi is known as a peacemaker. When one town went to war against another, Francis helped them come to a peaceful agreement. Francis wrote a prayer for peace. He wrote, "Lord, make me an instrument of your peace." For more about saints, visit "Lives of the Saints" at **www.webelieveweb.com**.

↳ **DISCIPLE CHALLENGE** Be a peacemaker. Pray the words of Saint Francis today.

Reality Check

Check the things someone should ask God's forgiveness for.

❏ being rude

❏ being unkind

❏ being selfish

❏ being happy

Take Home →

Talk with your family about the Sacrament of Penance. Write three important things you have learned that you will share with them.

_____

_____

_____

As a family, you might plan to visit your parish to celebrate the Sacrament of Penance.

CHAPTER TEST

Draw a line to match the sentence parts.

1. Absolution is •   • a prayer or kind act we do to make up for our sins.

2. A penance is •   • telling our sins to the priest.

3. Confession is •   • God's forgiveness of our sins by the priest.

4. Contrition is •   • being sorry for our sins and promising not to sin again.

Underline the correct answer.

5. Contrition, confession, a penance, and absolution are **(always, sometimes)** part of the Sacrament of Penance.

6. We **(always, sometimes)** gather with our parish community to celebrate the Sacrament of Penance together.

7. Jesus wants us to forgive others **(always, sometimes)**.

8. In the Sacrament of Penance, the priest **(always, sometimes)** forgives us in the name of Jesus.

9–10. Write two ways you can be a peacemaker.

"In his love Christ has filled us with joy as we prepare to celebrate his birth."

Advent I I Preface, Eucharistic Prayer

This chapter prepares us to celebrate the season of Advent.

Advent is a season of waiting and preparing.

WE GATHER

🎵 **Stay Awake**

Stay awake, be ready.
You do not know the hour when the
  Lord is coming.
Stay awake, be ready.
The Lord is coming soon!
Alleluia, alleluia!
The Lord is coming soon!

WE BELIEVE

The season of Advent is a time to prepare
to celebrate the coming of Jesus.
During Advent we watch and wait.

We watch for signs of God's love in the
world. We can see signs of God's love in:

- the gifts of his creation
- the loving ways people treat one another
- the work of the Church.

Think about some other signs of God's
love. Talk about them.

Jesus is the greatest sign of God's love.
Jesus is the Son of God who came into
the world. Jesus brings life and light to
all people.

The four weeks of Advent are filled with joy and hope. We celebrate this season at home and in our parish. One way of celebrating is by gathering around an Advent wreath. This wreath is made of evergreen branches and has four candles. There is one candle for each week of Advent. We pray as we light the candles each week.

Week One

 On the first Sunday of Advent we light the first purple candle.

 On the second Sunday of Advent we light the first and second purple candles.

Week Two

 On the third Sunday of Advent we light the first and second purple candles and the rose candle.

 On the fourth Sunday of Advent we light all four candles.

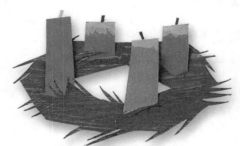

Week Three

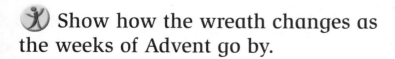 Show how the wreath changes as the weeks of Advent go by.

We light the Advent wreath to remind us to watch and wait for the coming of Jesus. The light from the candles reminds us that Jesus is the Light of the World.

Week Four

WE RESPOND

Jesus asks us to share his light with others. During the season of Advent, we can help people to see God's love.

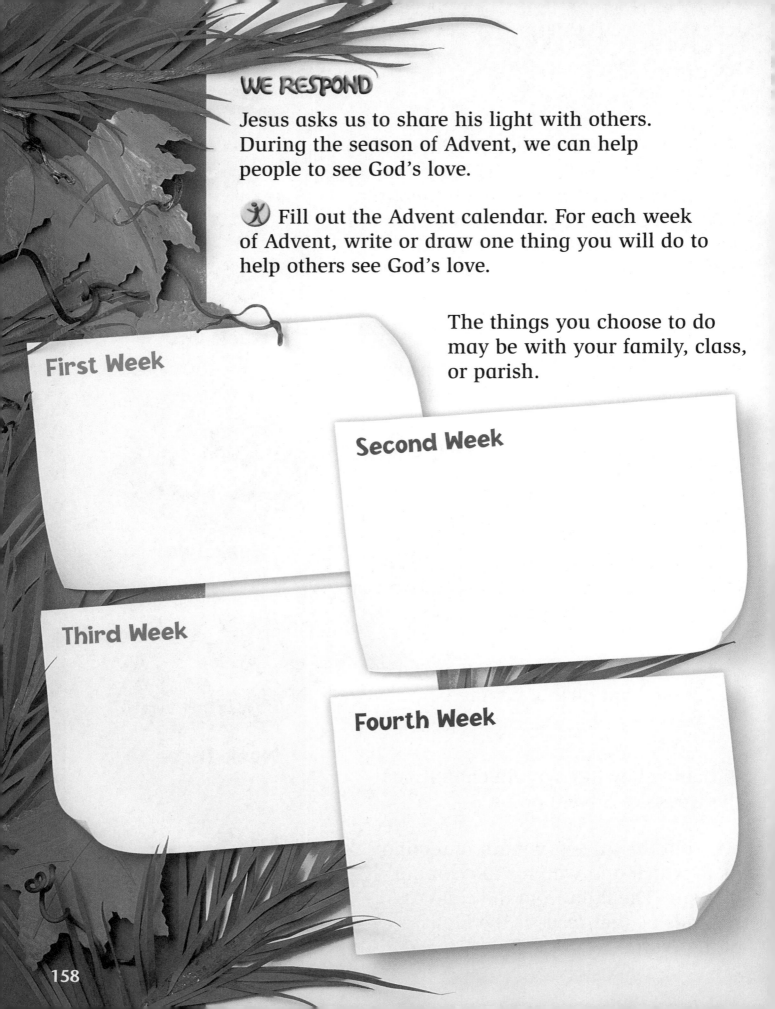 Fill out the Advent calendar. For each week of Advent, write or draw one thing you will do to help others see God's love.

The things you choose to do may be with your family, class, or parish.

First Week

Second Week

Third Week

Fourth Week

✝ We Respond in Prayer

Leader: Praised be the God of joy and hope.

All: Jesus, you are the Light of the World.

Leader: Let us listen to a reading from the Old Testament.

"The people who walked in darkness
have seen a great light." (Isaiah 9:1)

The word of the Lord.

All: Thanks be to God.

Leader: Let us pray. To our hearts and to our homes,

All: Come, Lord Jesus!

Leader: To our families and friends,

All: Come, Lord Jesus!

Leader: To people everywhere,

All: Come, Lord Jesus!

Leader: Let us walk in the light of Jesus!

All: Come, Lord Jesus!

Pray
Learn
Celebrate
Share
Choose
Live

Grade 2 Advent
PROJECT DISCIPLE

Picture This

Something is wrong with one of these pictures! Circle the picture that is correct.

↰ **DISCIPLE CHALLENGE** Which week of Advent is this

wreath celebrating? _____

Make it Happen

Write a postcard to another disciple to tell him or her what you learned about Advent. Include how you will celebrate Advent.

Take Home

With your family use these words to write your own prayer for Advent. Pray it together.

light   **Advent**

                prepare

wreath   **candle**

"Glory to God in the highest."

Luke 2:14

SEASONAL

CHAPTER 14

This chapter addresses the entire
Christmas season.

Christmas is a season to give glory to God.

WE GATHER

Who are the people you celebrate Christmas with? Who do you think about when you celebrate?

WE BELIEVE

During the Christmas season, we celebrate something wonderful. We celebrate God's greatest gift to us, his Son, Jesus. We give glory to God for the birth of Jesus.

 Act out this Christmas play.

 Luke 2:1–20

Narrator: During that time before Jesus' birth, a new rule was made. All men had to go back to the town of their father's family. They had to sign a list and be counted.

Joseph was from Bethlehem, the city of David. So Joseph had to go to Bethlehem with Mary.

"While they were there, the time came for her to have her child, and she gave birth to her firstborn son. She wrapped him in swaddling clothes and laid him in a manger, because there was no room for them in the inn." (Luke 2:6–7)

On the hills nearby, some shepherds were watching their sheep.

Shepherds: Look! Look! The sky is filled with light!

Narrator: All of a sudden, an angel appeared. The shepherds were afraid.

Angel: "Do not be afraid; for behold, I proclaim to you good news of great joy that will be for all the people. For today in the city of David a savior has been born for you who is Messiah and Lord. You will find an infant wrapped in swaddling clothes and lying in a manger." (Luke 2:10–12)

Narrator: Suddenly, many angels were there. They were all praising God and saying:

All Angels: "Glory to God in the highest." (Luke 2:14)

Narrator: The shepherds hurried to Bethlehem. They found Mary and Joseph, and the baby lying in the manger. The shepherds told them what the angels had said about this child. All were amazed. The shepherds went back to their fields, saying:

Shepherds: Praise God! Glory and praise to God forever! Amen!

The Christmas season lasts about two weeks. It begins on Christmas Day, December 25. The special color of the Christmas season is white. White is a color of light and joy. You will see this color during the celebration of the Mass.

During the Christmas season, we celebrate that Jesus is the Light of the World. He is with us now and forever.

We remember this all during the season, especially when we take part in Mass.

WE RESPOND

Decorate this banner.
Who will you share this Good News with?
How will you share it?

Jesus is with us Now and Forever

✝ We Respond in Prayer

Leader: Blessed be the name of the Lord.

All: Now and for ever.

Leader: Lord our God,
we praise you for the light of creation:
the sun, the moon, and the stars of
the night.

We praise you for Jesus Christ, your Son:
he is Emmanuel, God-with-us,
the Prince of Peace,
who fills us with the wonder of
your love.

All: We praise you, Lord God.

🎵 O Come, All Ye Faithful

O come, all ye faithful,
joyful and triumphant,
O come ye, O come ye to Bethlehem;
Come and behold him,
born the King of angels;

O come, let us adore him,
O come, let us adore him,
O come, let us adore him,
Christ, the Lord!

Pray
Learn
Celebrate
Share
Choose
Live

Grade 2 Christmas
PROJECT DISCIPLE

Celebrate! Draw a picture story about Jesus' birth.

Mary and Joseph went to Bethlehem.

Jesus was laid in a manger.

Shepherds visited Jesus.

Pray Today

The Christmas season is a good time to bless your home.

Lord, Creator of heaven and earth, bless our home.
Make it a place of peace and love.
Amen.

Take Home

Talk about ways you can fill your home with peace and love during the Christmas season.

Fill in the circle beside the correct answer.

1. God will _____ forgive us if we are sorry.
   - ○ sometimes
   - ○ never
   - ○ always

2. _____ is God's forgiveness of our sins by the priest in the Sacrament of Penance.
   - ○ Absolution
   - ○ Celebration
   - ○ Contrition

3. God's gift that allows us to make choices is _____.
   - ○ penance
   - ○ free will
   - ○ mercy

4. The _____ Testament is the part of the Bible about Jesus and the beginning of the Church.
   - ○ New
   - ○ Old
   - ○ Free

Draw a line to match the sentence parts.

5. The Act of Contrition •

6. The Great Commandment •

7. God's gift of conscience •

• helps us to know right from wrong.

• is a prayer of sorrow.

• is Jesus' teaching to love God and one another.

continued on next page   167

8. **Write a sentence to tell what you have learned about the Ten Commandments.**

_____

_____

_____ .

9. **Look at the photograph. Write two different things that the child can choose to do.**

The child could choose to

_____

_____

_____

_____ .

10. **Circle the choice Jesus would want the child to make.**

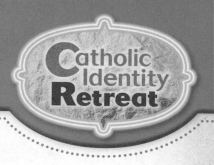
The Sacrament of the Eucharist

Part 1 I Open My Heart

At Mass we recall Jesus' sacrifice of himself for us, given to us in the Eucharist. The altar reminds us that the Mass is a holy meal since it is a remembrance of the holy meal Jesus shared at the Last Supper.

Look at the altar in the picture. Think about being at Mass.

How is the Mass like sharing a meal at a table with friends or family?

_____

_____

_____

_____

_____

_____

The Sacrament of the Eucharist

Part 2 We Come Together for Prayer

Leader: Lord Jesus, your love for us is so great. You gave us the gift of yourself in the Eucharist. When we receive the Eucharist, we "are united more closely to Christ" (*CCC*, 1396). Jesus, prepare us to be united with you.

All: Lord, fill our hearts with your love.

Reader 1: Jesus, you invite us to your table, to receive the gift of your Body and Blood.

All: Lord, fill our hearts with your love.

Reader 2: Jesus, your love for us never ends.

All: Lord, fill our hearts with your love.

Leader: Jesus, help us to always have your love in our hearts. Help us to . . . (*Add your own request to Jesus. Pray it aloud.*)

All: Lord, fill our hearts with your love. Amen.

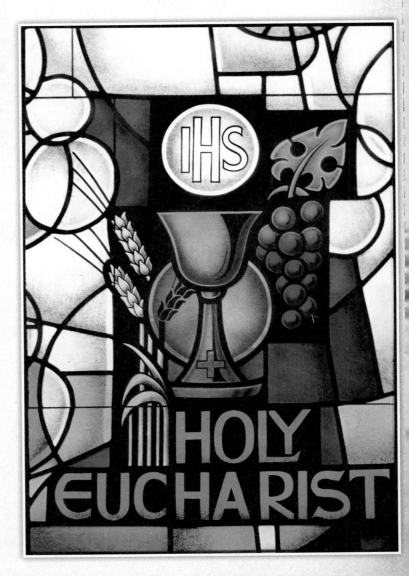

The Sacrament of the Eucharist

Part 3 I Cherish God's Word

"Jesus said to them, 'I am the bread of life; whoever comes to me will never hunger, and whoever believes in me will never thirst.'" (John 6:35)

READ the Scripture passage. Read slowly. Pay close attention to what you are reading.

REFLECT on what you read. Think about:

- What does it feel like to be hungry or thirsty?

- What does "bread of life" mean to you?

- How can you prepare your heart to receive Jesus in Holy Communion?

SHARE your thoughts and feelings with God in prayer. Let your thoughts and feelings come naturally. Speak to God as a friend.

CONTEMPLATE or sit quietly and think about God's Word in the Scripture passage from the Gospel of John above.

The Miracle of the Loaves and Fishes, by Harold Copping (1863–1932)

The Sacrament of the Eucharist

Part 4   I Value My Catholic Faith

At the Last Supper, Jesus gave us the gift of his Body and Blood. During the Mass we remember what Jesus did at the Last Supper.

Work in groups to compare the events of the Last Supper to what happens at Mass.

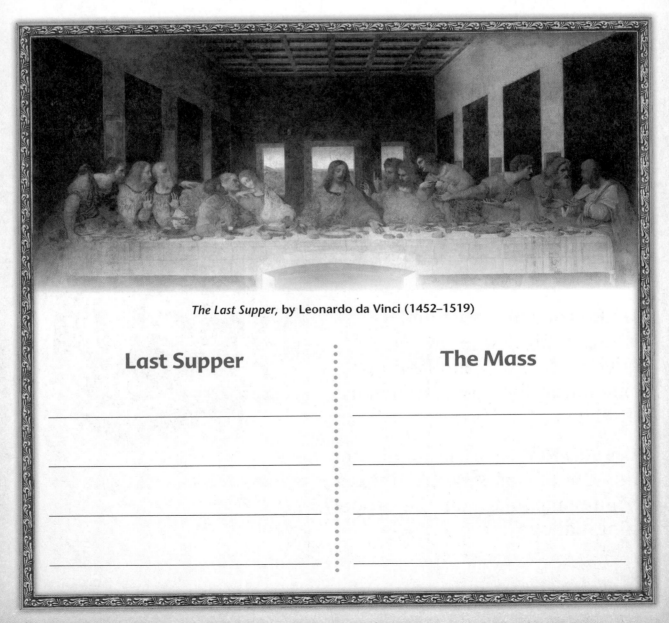

The Last Supper, by Leonardo da Vinci (1452–1519)

Last Supper	The Mass

The Sacrament of the Eucharist

Part 5 I Celebrate Catholic Identity

In each circle, write a way you can thank Jesus for the gift of the Eucharist. Copy your favorite three ways onto the banner circles you were given. Now string all the circles together. Hang up the finished banner in the classroom or parish hall. This banner will remind us to say thank-you to Jesus.

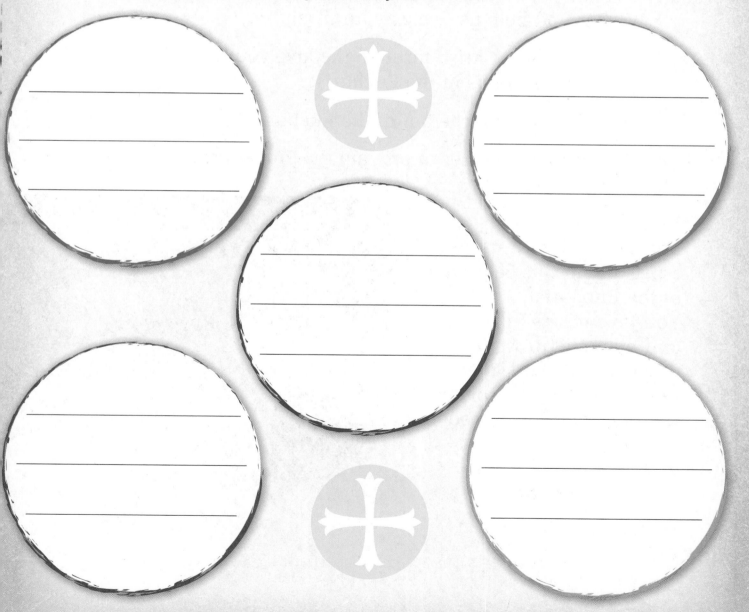

The Sacrament of the Eucharist

Part 6 I Honor My Catholic Identity

All: Lord, thank you for the gift of the Eucharist.

Reader 1: "Then he took the bread, said the blessing, broke it, and gave it to them, saying, 'This is my body, which will be given for you; do this in memory of me.'" (Luke 22:19)

Leader: Let us pray. Jesus, in the Eucharist, you take away our hunger and help us live as your disciples.

Reader 2: Lord Jesus Christ, through the love you have for us, you give yourself to us in the Eucharist.

All: Lord, thank you for the gift of the Eucharist.

Leader: Let us join together in praying the Prayer before the Blessed Sacrament.

All: Jesus,
You are God-with-us,
especially in this Sacrament
of the Eucharist.
You love me as I am
and help me grow.
Come and be with me
in all my joys and sorrows.
Help me share your peace
    and love
with everyone I meet.
I ask in your name.
Amen.

Child receiving First Holy Communion from Pope Francis

Bringing the Retreat Home

The Sacrament of the Eucharist

Retreat Recap

Review the pages of your child's *Celebrating Catholic Identity: Liturgy & Sacraments* retreat. Ask your child to tell you about the retreat. Talk about the Sacrament of the Eucharist:

- The Eucharist is the Sacrament of the Body and Blood of Jesus Christ.

- Jesus gives us the gift of himself in the Eucharist. We receive this gift of Jesus in Holy Communion.

- The Eucharist helps us to live as Jesus' disciples.

A True Gift

The Eucharist is truly a gift in our lives. At Mass, the gifts of bread and wine are offered, and these gifts become the Body and Blood of Christ. This happens by the power of the Holy Spirit and through the words and actions of the priest. Then we receive Jesus himself in Holy Communion. Share with your child memories of your First Holy Communion Day, or one you have attended. Write an important memory of this day below.

Take a Moment

The Blessed Sacrament is another name for the Eucharist. Contact your parish to ask when Adoration of the Blessed Sacrament is offered. Attend as a family, praying and meditating together on the presence of Jesus Christ in the Eucharist.

Family Prayer

Review this prayer as a family. You may wish to silently pray these words when you receive Holy Communion.

Jesus, you are the bread of life.
Thank you for sharing your life with me.
Help me always to be your friend and disciple.

For more resources, see the *Catholic Identity Home Companion* at the end of this book.

Why We Believe
As a Catholic Family

What if someone asks us:

- What do Catholics believe about the Eucharist?

The following resources can help us to respond:

Jesus instituted the Sacrament of the Eucharist at the Last Supper, the meal Jesus shared with his disciples before he died. "Jesus took bread, said the blessing, broke it, and giving it to his disciples said, 'Take and eat; this is my body.' Then he took a cup, gave thanks, and gave it to them, saying, 'Drink from it, all of you, for this is my blood of the covenant, which will be shed on behalf of many for the forgiveness of sins.'" (Matthew 26:26–28) Jesus told his disciples that the bread and wine were his Body and his Blood. He instructed them to continue to do this in memory of him.

In the Sacrament of the Eucharist, the priest does and says what Jesus said and did at the Last Supper. The priest takes the bread and says:

"TAKE THIS, ALL OF YOU, AND EAT OF IT,
FOR THIS IS MY BODY, WHICH WILL BE GIVEN UP FOR YOU."

Then the priest takes the cup of wine and says:
"TAKE THIS, ALL OF YOU, AND DRINK
FROM IT, FOR THIS IS THE CHALICE OF MY BLOOD. . . ."

This is called the *Consecration*. Through the words and actions of the priest, and by the power of the Holy Spirit, the bread and wine are changed into the Body and Blood of Christ. What looks and tastes like bread and wine has become the Body and Blood of Christ.

🌿 What does Scripture say?

"The cup of blessing that we bless, is it not a participation in the blood of Christ? The bread that we break, is it not a participation in the body of Christ?" (1 Corinthians 10:16)

In the Eucharist, the Body and Blood, together with the soul and divinity, of our Lord Jesus Christ become present to us. In the Eucharist we receive the fullness of Jesus poured out for us on the Cross and first offered at the Last Supper. He is our Bread of Life, given so that we might have eternal life. The Eucharist is the greatest gift Jesus Christ leaves to us!

The true presence of Jesus Christ in the Eucharist under the appearances of bread and wine is called the Real Presence. When we receive Holy Communion, we remember that Jesus is truly present.

🌿 What does the Church say?

"The Council of Trent summarizes the Catholic faith by declaring: 'Because Christ our Redeemer said that it was truly his body that he was offering under the species of bread, it has always been the conviction of the Church of God, and this holy Council now declares again, that by the consecration of the bread and wine there takes place a change of the whole substance of the bread into the substance of the body of Christ our Lord and of the whole substance of the wine into the substance of his blood. This change the holy Catholic Church has fittingly and properly called transubstantiation.'" (Catechism of the Catholic Church, 1376)

Notes:

Jesus Gives Himself in the Eucharist

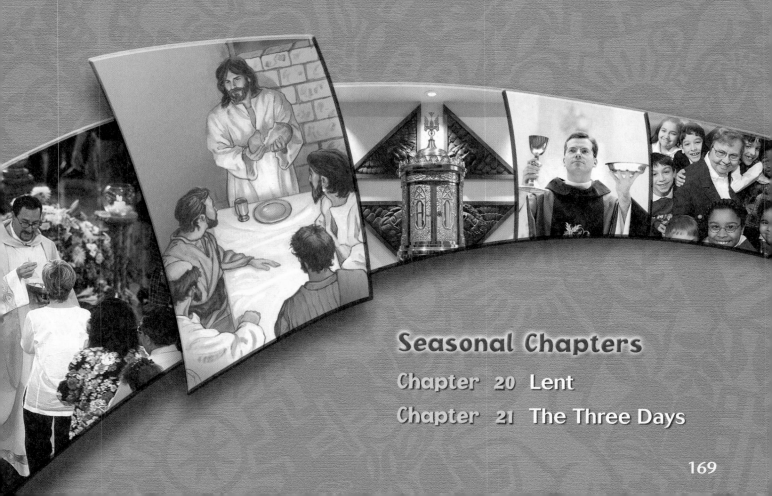

Seasonal Chapters

PROJECT DISCIPLE
DEAR FAMILY

In Unit 3 your child will grow as a disciple of Jesus by:

- appreciating that Jesus gave us the gift of himself at the Last Supper
- gathering at Mass to celebrate what Jesus did at the Last Supper
- listening to God's Word during the Liturgy of the Word
- recognizing that Jesus is truly present in the Eucharist
- sharing God's love and peace with others.

What's the Word?

In Chapter 15, the children hear the Scripture story of Jesus feeding the crowd of people. Read the story together from the Bible (John 6:1–14), or retell it in your own words. Point out that it was a child who offered the five barley loaves and two fish. With the loaves and fish, Jesus performed a miracle and fed thousands of people. What are some ways that children help others today? Affirm your child's talents and abilities, and suggest ways to use those talents to help others. Remind your child that we hear stories from the Bible every Sunday at Mass during the Liturgy of the Word.

Picture This

Look at the photos of the celebration of the Mass on pages 188–191. Talk about your own parish celebration of Mass. How does your church look the same or different from the photos? How do the people in your parish participate in the Mass? Decide on one way your family will participate more fully this Sunday.

Reality Check

"Parents have the mission of teaching their children to pray and to discover their vocation as children of God."

(Catechism of the Catholic Church, 2226)

Celebrate!

Make your next family meal a special one—maybe by serving a favorite food or dessert, or eating "picnic" style in the family room. Talk about how sharing a meal brings us closer together and how Jesus must have felt when he shared the Last Supper with his friends. Use this as an opportunity to build your child's anticipation of receiving first Holy Communion.

Make it Happen

After Mass on Sunday point out the tabernacle to your child. Pray together to Jesus in the Blessed Sacrament. As you leave the church, talk about one thing you will do together to share God's love. Do it!

Take Home

Each chapter in your child's *We Believe* Grade 2 text offers a "Take Home" activity that invites your family to support your child's journey to more fully become a disciple of Christ.

Be ready for this unit's Take Home:

Chapter 15: Preparing and sharing a family meal

Chapter 16: Participating at Mass

Chapter 17: Praying for the needs of others

Chapter 18: Presenting the gifts at Mass

Chapter 19: Promoting peace in the family

Jesus Gives Us the Eucharist

✝ We Gather in Prayer

🎵 We Remember You

Jesus, we remember you.
Jesus, we remember you.
We remember you gave your life for us.
We remember. We believe.

We praise you, we remember you.
We bless you, we remember you,
and we thank you that we belong to you.
We remember. We believe.

Jesus brings us life.

WE GATHER

✠ *Jesus, you give us all we need.*

What kind of food do people make with wheat? Why is this food important?

WE BELIEVE

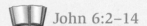 Act out the following story. It tells about a time when Jesus fed many hungry people.

📖 John 6:2–14

Reader: One day thousands of people were listening to Jesus. He saw that the sun was setting. He knew that the people were hungry. Jesus asked Philip where they could find enough food for all these people.

Philip: Jesus, we could never find enough food to feed this many people!

Andrew: There is a boy here who has five loaves of bread and two fish.

Reader: Jesus took the loaves and gave thanks. He asked his disciples to give out the bread and fish. There was enough food to feed everyone. And when the people were done eating, there was food left over. So Jesus asked the disciples to gather this food.

Disciples: Look, there are still twelve baskets filled with food!

All: What a wonderful thing Jesus has done for us!

Jesus told us, "I am the living bread that came down from heaven; whoever eats this bread will live forever." (John 6:51)

All of us need bread to live and grow. All of us need Jesus to grow closer to God and share in God's life. Jesus is the living bread. He is the Son of God who was sent to bring us life.

WE RESPOND

How can we grow closer to Jesus? How can we help others to grow closer to Jesus?

Pray to Jesus and ask him to help you to grow closer to God.

173

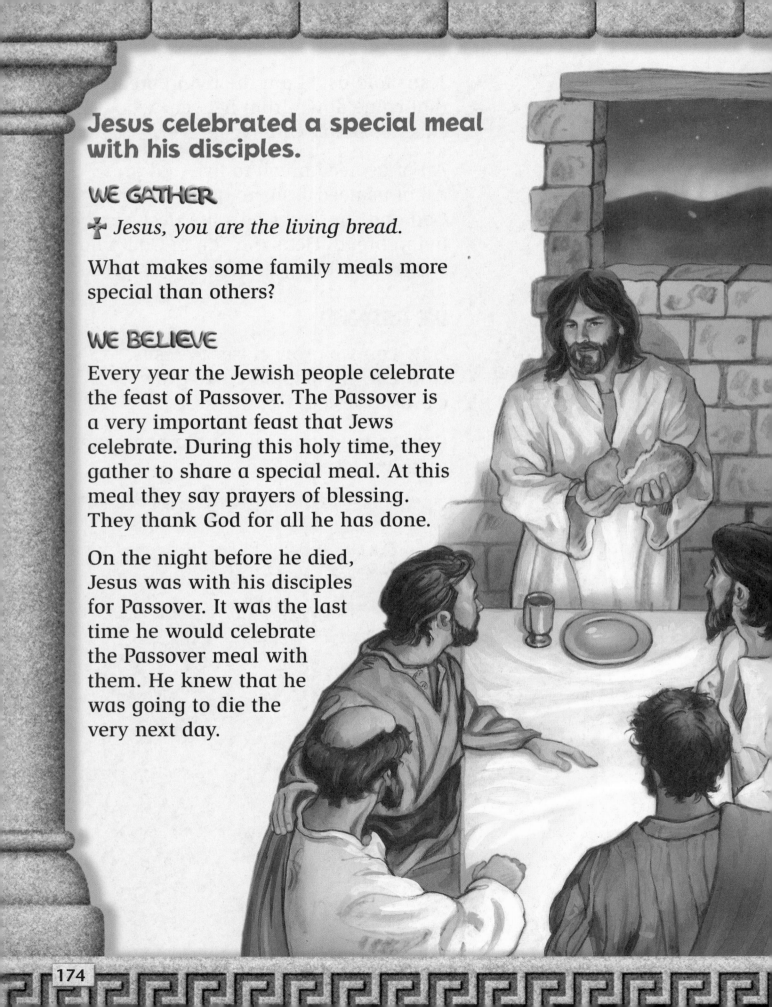

Jesus celebrated a special meal with his disciples.

WE GATHER

✝ *Jesus, you are the living bread.*

What makes some family meals more special than others?

WE BELIEVE

Every year the Jewish people celebrate the feast of Passover. The Passover is a very important feast that Jews celebrate. During this holy time, they gather to share a special meal. At this meal they say prayers of blessing. They thank God for all he has done.

On the night before he died, Jesus was with his disciples for Passover. It was the last time he would celebrate the Passover meal with them. He knew that he was going to die the very next day.

Here is what happened at the meal.

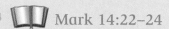 Mark 14:22–24

During the meal Jesus took bread and said a blessing. He broke the bread and gave it to his disciples. He said, "Take it; this is my body."
(Mark 14:22)

Then Jesus took a cup of wine and gave thanks. All the disciples drank from this cup. Jesus said, "This is my blood." (Mark 14:24)

The meal Jesus shared with his disciples on the night before he died is called the **Last Supper**. At this meal the bread and wine became the Body and Blood of Jesus Christ.

Key Word

Last Supper the meal Jesus shared with his disciples on the night before he died

Fill out this chart to help you remember what Jesus said and did at the Last Supper.

Jesus' Actions	Jesus' Words
_____	_____
_____	_____
_____	_____

WE RESPOND

Why was the Last Supper a special meal?

As followers of Jesus, when do we share special meals together?

In the Eucharist we remember and celebrate what Jesus did at the Last Supper.

WE GATHER

✞ *Jesus, thank you for giving yourself to us.*

What are some special events that you remember? Why does remembering them make you happy?

WE BELIEVE

At the Last Supper Jesus told the disciples to remember what he had just done. Jesus wanted them to remember and celebrate this special meal again and again. Jesus said, "Do this in memory of me."
(Luke 22:19)

The Church continues to remember and celebrate what Jesus did at the Last Supper. We do as Jesus asked when we celebrate the Eucharist.

The **Eucharist** is the sacrament of the Body and Blood of Jesus Christ. In this sacrament, the bread and wine become the Body and Blood of Christ.

> **Key Word**
>
> **Eucharist** the sacrament of the Body and Blood of Jesus Christ

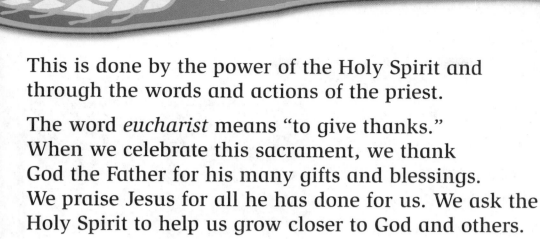

This is done by the power of the Holy Spirit and through the words and actions of the priest.

The word *eucharist* means "to give thanks." When we celebrate this sacrament, we thank God the Father for his many gifts and blessings. We praise Jesus for all he has done for us. We ask the Holy Spirit to help us grow closer to God and others.

WE RESPOND

What gifts has God given to your class? How can your class thank God for these gifts?

Name gifts that God has given you. What can you do this week to show that you are thankful for God's gifts? Draw or write your answer.

The Mass is a meal and a sacrifice.

WE GATHER

✝ *Holy Spirit, help us grow closer to God.*

🕴 Act out each story. Tell what is different about the meals.

- Gema is late for soccer practice. She quickly eats a sandwich.

- It is Gema's dad's birthday. All of Gema's family are coming over to celebrate. They will have a birthday dinner.

WE BELIEVE

The celebration of the Eucharist is called the **Mass**. During the Mass we gather together to listen to God's Word and receive the Body and Blood of Christ.

The Mass is a meal. During the Mass we remember what Jesus did at the Last Supper. The bread and wine become the Body and Blood of Christ. **Holy Communion** is receiving the Body and Blood of Christ. Holy Communion makes the life of God within us stronger.

The Mass is a sacrifice. A *sacrifice* is an offering of a gift to God. The word *offer* means "to give" or "to present." Jesus offered the greatest sacrifice of all time. He died on the cross to save us from sin and to bring us new life.

As Catholics...

Every Catholic church has an altar. At the altar the sacrifice of Jesus is made present.

The altar is a table and it reminds us of the table of the Last Supper. From this table we receive Jesus in Holy Communion.

Think about the church where your parish community gathers for Mass. Where is the altar? What does the altar look like?

At every Mass we remember Jesus' sacrifice. We remember that Jesus gave himself so that we might have life.

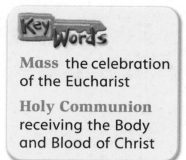

When we take part in the Mass, we remember and celebrate that:

- Jesus offered his life for us on the cross. He died to save us from sin.

- Jesus rose to new life so that we could live happily with God forever.

- Jesus gives us his own Body and Blood in Holy Communion. He gives us himself.

WE RESPOND

Look at the pictures below. What can each picture help you to remember about the Mass?

PROJECT

Show What *you* Know

Fill in each card.

 The meal that Jesus shared with his disciples on the night before he died is the

_____

 The sacrament of the Body and Blood of Jesus Christ is the

_____

 Receiving the Body and Blood of Christ is

_____

Key Word The celebration of the Eucharist is called the

_____

Pray Today

This prayer is called *Grace Before Meals*. You can pray it before you enjoy a meal.

Decorate the frame.

Pray this prayer with your family and friends.

> *Bless us, O Lord, and these your gifts which we are about to receive from your goodness, through Christ, our Lord. Amen.*

DISC1PLE

Pray
Learn
Celebrate
Share
Choose
Live

Reality Check

In the Bible, we read that Jesus fed many hungry people. We can follow Jesus' example. Check the ways that you and your family can help other families who are hungry.

❏ Give to food collections

❏ Try not to waste food

❏ Help out at your parish soup kitchen

❏ Pray for those people who are hungry

❏ Another way: _____

PARISH KITCHEN

Make *it* Happen

Before Mass, talk with your family. Explain that the Mass is a meal and a sacrifice.

Take Home

This week, make one of your family meals a special celebration. Together, plan the menu and decorations.

Menu

_____

_____

Decorations

_____

_____

Ask each family member to help prepare for the meal in some way. Then, before your meal, pray the *Grace Before Meals*.

CHAPTER TEST

Use the words in the box to complete the sentences.

1. The word *eucharist* means to

   _____.

2. The _____ is the
   celebration of the Eucharist.

3. Jesus wants us to _____
   and celebrate what he did at the Last
   Supper.

4. The Mass is a _____
   and a sacrifice.

5. A _____ is an offering of a gift to God.

6. _____ is receiving the Body and Blood
   of Christ.

remember
meal
sacrifice
Mass
give thanks
Holy Communion

7–8. What did Jesus do at the Last Supper?

_____

_____

9–10. What do we remember and celebrate at every Mass?

_____

_____

✝ We Gather in Prayer

Leader: Join hands to form a circle. Let us listen to God's Word.

Reader: Jesus said, "For where two or three are gathered in my name, there am I in the midst of them." (Matthew 18:20)

Leader: Jesus, we gather in your name. Together we thank God our Father for his many gifts.

All: God our Father, we thank you.

Leader: Jesus, we gather in your name. Together we praise you for all you have done for us.

All: God the Son, we praise you.

Leader: Jesus, we gather in your name. Together we ask the Holy Spirit to help us to grow closer to God and to others.

All: God the Holy Spirit, help us.

We are united to Jesus Christ and to one another.

WE GATHER

✝ *Jesus, we come together in your name.*

 Look at the picture of the grapevine. Circle where each branch is joined to the vine. Trace the way the food and water from the soil get to each of the branches.

WE BELIEVE

At the Last Supper, Jesus talked to his disciples about many things. One thing he told them was that he would always be with them.

Jesus also told them to stay close to him and to one another. He said, "I am the vine. You are the branches." (John 15:5) He told them that they were joined to him and one another as branches are joined to a vine.

Jesus wanted his disciples to work and pray together. He wanted them to share God's love with the whole world.

We are Jesus' disciples, too. Jesus is with us always. Each time we come together to celebrate the sacraments, he is with us. When we celebrate the Sacrament of the Eucharist, Jesus is with us in a special way. He gives himself to us. We receive the bread and wine that have become the Body and Blood of Christ. We who receive Holy Communion are united to Jesus and to one another. Through Holy Communion our venial sins are forgiven and we are helped to avoid serious sin.

WE RESPOND

How can you stay close to Jesus? How can you share God's love with your family, friends, and the world?

Join hands and pray together. Jesus, you are the vine. We are the branches. You give yourself to us as food in the Eucharist. Help us to grow in love for God and others.

The Church celebrates the Mass.

WE GATHER

✝ *Jesus, you are the vine and we are the branches.*

Why is Sunday a special day?

WE BELIEVE

Sunday is a special day for the Church. Sunday is also called the *Lord's Day*. This is because Jesus Christ rose to new life on this day. Every Sunday Catholics gather in their parishes. Together with their parish priest they celebrate the Mass.

The Mass is the greatest way to worship God. This is why the Church tells us to take part in the Mass every Sunday of the year. We can also celebrate the Sunday Mass on Saturday evening.

During Mass we gather as a community to:

• praise and thank God

• listen to God's Word

• remember and celebrate Jesus' life, Death, and Resurrection

• celebrate Jesus' gift of himself in the Eucharist.

At the end of Mass we are sent out to live as Jesus taught us.

As Catholics...

One of the laws of the Church is that we must take part in the Mass every Sunday and on other special days. These other special days are called *holy days of obligation*. An obligation is a requirement.

In many places, Mass is celebrated each day of the week. We are invited to take part in Mass every day.

How does taking part in the Mass help us to live as Jesus taught us?

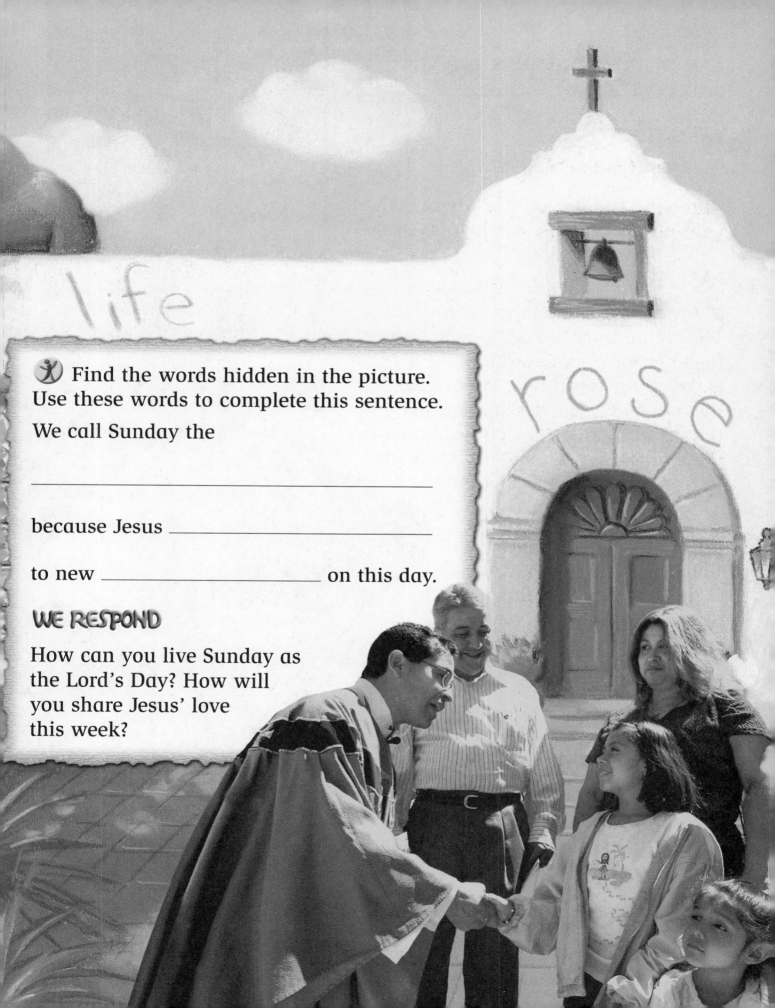

life

rose

👤 Find the words hidden in the picture. Use these words to complete this sentence.

We call Sunday the

_____

because Jesus _____

to new _____ on this day.

WE RESPOND

How can you live Sunday as the Lord's Day? How will you share Jesus' love this week?

The parish gathers for the celebration of Mass.

WE GATHER

✝ *God, we gather together to praise you.*

Name the people you usually see when your parish gathers to celebrate Mass.

WE BELIEVE

Many people come together for Mass. The community of people who join together for the celebration of the Mass is called the **assembly**. We are part of the assembly. The assembly gives thanks and praise to God throughout the whole celebration. A priest leads the assembly in this celebration.

Sometimes a deacon takes part in the celebration of the Mass. When a deacon is present, he reads the Gospel during Mass. He prays some special prayers. He also helps the priest at the altar.

The priest offers our prayers to God. He does what Jesus did at the Last Supper.

Altar servers do many things to help the priest and deacon. Readers read the first two Bible readings. Extraordinary ministers of Holy Communion help give out Holy Communion.

Key Word

assembly the community of people who join together for the celebration of the Mass

After Mass, the extraordinary ministers of Holy Communion may bring Holy Communion to those who are sick or not able to be at Mass.

WE RESPOND

What can you do to participate at Mass now? What can you do to participate at Mass as you get older?

When Mass begins, we praise God and ask for his forgiveness.

WE GATHER

✝ *May the Lord be with us today.*

How do you take part in a special celebration?

WE BELIEVE

When we join together at Mass, we show God our love and thanks. It is important for each person in the assembly to take part in the celebration.

The beginning of the Mass unites us as members of the Church. It prepares us to hear God's Word and to celebrate the Eucharist.

Here are the ways we take part as Mass begins.

- We greet other members of the community.

- We stand and sing to praise God as a community. As we sing, the priest, deacon, and others helping at Mass walk to the altar.

- We make the Sign of the Cross. This reminds us of our Baptism.

- The priest prays,
  "The Lord be with you."
  We respond,
  "And with your spirit."
  This helps us to know that Jesus is present with us.

- We ask God and one another for forgiveness.

- We ask for God's mercy. We may pray with the priest:
  "Lord, have mercy."
  "Christ, have mercy."
  "Lord, have mercy."

- We sing or say together a prayer of praise. This prayer begins with these words.
  "Glory to God in the highest, and on earth peace to people of good will."

- The priest says an opening prayer. We respond,
  "Amen."

WE RESPOND

What are some ways you take part in the beginning of the Mass?

🎵 God Is Here!

God is here! Come, let us celebrate!
God is here! Let us rejoice!
God is here! Come, let us celebrate!
God is here! Let us rejoice!

PROJECT

Show What *you* Know

yamselsb

Unscramble the 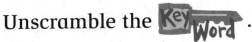 . _____

Draw what the word means.

Picture This

Finish the web.

We listen to
_____.

We celebrate
_____.

AT MASS

We praise
_____.

We remember
_____.

DISCIPLE

Pray
Learn
Celebrate
Share
Choose
Live

Make *it* Happen

In many parishes, there are people who welcome us to the celebration of Mass. These people greet us as we enter the church. Their words help us to feel welcome and to know that we belong to the Church. We should greet one another, too. Greeting one another is a good way to prepare for the celebration of the Eucharist. What is one way you will greet someone at the celebration of Mass this Sunday?

Fast Facts

For many years, the Church celebrated Mass only in the Latin language. Today, some parishes offer Latin Masses.

↳ **DISCIPLE CHALLENGE**

Go to Latin Hall at **www.weliveourfaith.com**.

Listen to the Sign of the Cross in Latin.

Take Home

This Sunday, pay close attention to what happens at Mass. Talk about what your family does to take part in Mass. Write one thing on each line below.

_____

_____

_____

CHAPTER TEST

Check the things we do at the beginning of Mass.

1. ____ We receive Holy Communion.

2. ____ We ask God for forgiveness.

3. ____ We stand and sing.

4. ____ We prepare to hear God's Word.

Fill in the circle beside the correct answer.

5. It is important for _____ in the assembly to take part in the celebration of Mass.
   ○ only children   ○ each person

6. Glory to God is a prayer of _____.
   ○ praise   ○ sorrow

7. The _____ leads the assembly at Mass.
   ○ priest   ○ deacon

8. The beginning of Mass _____ us as members of the Church.
   ○ divides   ○ unites

9–10. Write two reasons Catholics gather for Mass every Sunday.

_____

We Celebrate the Liturgy of the Word

✝ We Gather in Prayer

Leader: Let us pray.

🎵 **Alleluia, We Will Listen**

Alleluia, alleluia,
   we will listen to your word.
Alleluia! Alleluia!
We will listen. Alleluia!

Reader: A reading from the holy Gospel according to Luke.

"Afterward [Jesus] journeyed from one town and village to another, preaching and proclaiming the good news of the kingdom of God . . ."
(Luke 8:1)

The Gospel of the Lord.

All: Praise to you, Lord Jesus Christ.

We listen to God's Word during the Liturgy of the Word.

WE GATHER

✢ *O God, we will listen to your Word.*

You know the words to some stories and songs. How did you learn these words?

Unscramble these letters to complete this sentence.

e g i l n s t i n

Sometimes we learn by

l _ _ _ _ n _ _ _ .

WE BELIEVE

The Mass has two main parts. The first main part of the Mass is the **Liturgy of the Word**. During the Liturgy of the Word, we worship God by listening to his Word. We listen to readings from the Bible.

At Sunday Mass we usually hear three readings from the Bible. When we listen to these readings, we grow in faith. We hear about God's love for us. We learn ways to show our love for God and others.

God's Word has always been an important part of the Church's worship. We hear God's Word during the celebration of all the sacraments.

By listening to God's Word, we learn to be better followers of Jesus. We can learn to care for one another. As we listen and learn, we can grow in God's love.

WE RESPOND

How can listening to the Word of God help you grow in faith?

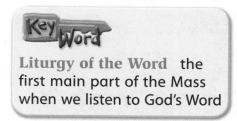 Work with a partner. Think of Bible stories that you remember. Tell the stories to one another. Talk about what each story means.

Key Word

Liturgy of the Word the first main part of the Mass when we listen to God's Word

We listen and respond to readings from the Old Testament and the New Testament.

WE GATHER

✝ *O God, your ways are ways of love.*

What does your family do to remember the people and events that are special to all of you?

WE BELIEVE

The Liturgy of the Word begins with the first reading. The first reading is usually from the Old Testament. We hear about all the great things God did for his people before Jesus was born. This helps us to remember that God has always been with his people. When we listen, we also know that God is with us now.

After the first reading we let God's Word enter our hearts. Then we sing a psalm. A **psalm** is a song of praise from the Bible. The leader of song or the reader prays a psalm verse. Then we sing or say a response.

Next we listen to the second reading. This is from the New Testament. It is about the teachings of the Apostles and the beginning of the Church.

psalm a song of praise from the Bible

The way of the Lord

The way of the Lord

When we listen to the second reading, we learn how to be followers of Jesus. We remember and give thanks that we are the Church.

At the end of the first and second readings, the reader says,
"The Word of the Lord."
We respond,
"Thanks be to God."

WE RESPOND

What can you do during the week to prepare for the readings at Mass?

♫ Make up a tune or special beat for this psalm response.

"Your ways, O Lord, are love and truth."

Sing or say these words often.

We listen as the Gospel is proclaimed.

WE GATHER

✝ *Praise to you, Lord Jesus Christ.*

We share good news with one another in a joyful way.

Act out how you would share this news.

- Grandfather is better. He is coming home from the hospital.
- Gabriella won first prize at the science fair.

WE BELIEVE

There are four books in the New Testament called Gospels: Matthew, Mark, Luke, and John. In these Gospels we learn the Good News about Jesus' life and teaching. The third reading of the Liturgy of the Word is from one of the Gospels.

The deacon or priest proclaims the Gospel. To proclaim the Gospel means to announce the Good News of Jesus Christ with praise and glory.

Alleluia!

This is what we do:

- We stand. We sing the alleluia or other words of praise. This shows we are ready to listen to the Good News of Jesus.

- We listen as the deacon or priest proclaims the Gospel.

- Then the deacon or priest says, "The Gospel of the Lord." We respond, "Praise to you, Lord Jesus Christ."

After the Gospel, the priest or deacon talks about the readings at Mass. In this talk he helps us to understand the readings. This talk is called the **homily**. Through the homily we learn what it means to believe and what we can do to be followers of Jesus. We learn how we can grow closer to God and to one another.

WE RESPOND

These are a few Gospel stories that we have shared in class. Talk about each story.

- Jesus tells the story of the lost sheep (Luke 15:1–7).

- Jesus invites people to follow him (Matthew 4:18–22).

- Jesus tells the story of the forgiving father (Luke 15:11–24).

 Draw a ☺ beside the story you like best. Tell why you like it.

Key Word

homily the talk given by the priest or deacon that helps us understand the readings and how we are to live

Together we pray the Creed and the Prayer of the Faithful.

WE GATHER

✝ *God, we believe in you.*

🎵 We Believe

We believe in God the Father,
We believe in God the Son,
We believe in God the Spirit;
God is three, and God is one.

WE BELIEVE

After the homily we stand to pray the Creed. In this prayer we show our faith. We say what we believe as Christians.

The word *creed* comes from a word that means "believe." Here are some of the words we say in the Creed.

- "I believe in one God,
    the Father almighty,
  maker of heaven and earth. . . ."

- "I believe in one Lord Jesus Christ,
    the Only Begotten Son of God. . . ."

- "I believe in the Holy Spirit, the Lord,
    the giver of life. . . ."

We also say that we believe in the Church and in God's forgiveness of our sins.

After the Creed, we pray for the needs of all God's people. This prayer is called the Prayer of the Faithful. During this prayer, we pray for:

- the whole Church
- the pope and bishops
- the world and all its leaders
- those who are sick or in need
- the people in our parish who have died
- people we know and for whom we want to pray
- ourselves and any needs we may have.

After each prayer, we ask God to hear our prayer.

WE RESPOND

Who would you like to pray for next Sunday at Mass?

Pray quietly for these people now.

PROJECT

Show What *you* Know

Use this color code to color the  .

 **red** — the first main part of the Mass when we listen to God's Word

 **blue** — a song of praise from the Bible

 **yellow** — the talk given by the priest or deacon that helps us understand the readings and how we are to live

psalm

Liturgy of the Word

homily

More *to* Explore

At Mass this Sunday, listen closely to the priest's or deacon's homily. Then ask yourself these questions. When did the homily take place? What did the priest or deacon say that helps me to live as a disciple?

DISCIPLE

Pray
Learn
Celebrate
Share
Choose
Live

Make *it* Happen

Help proclaim the Good News!
Write an advice column to other disciples about ways they can be like Jesus in their communities.

Dear Disciples,

Pray Today

Leaders of the world have great responsibilities. That is why it is important to pray for them. We pray together for them during the Prayer of the Faithful on Sunday. We can also pray for them at other times. Say a prayer now for world leaders.

Take Home

Lead your family members in this prayer. Have them say, "Lord, hear our prayer" after each part of the prayer.

For the whole Church,
For all those in our parish,
For those who are sick or in need,

↳ **DISCIPLE CHALLENGE** Add your own.

_____

205

CHAPTER TEST

Fill in the circle beside the correct answer.

1. The first reading at Mass is usually from the _____.
   ○ Old Testament   ○ New Testament

2. The second reading at Mass is usually from the _____.
   ○ Old Testament   ○ New Testament

3. In the _____ we say what we believe as Christians.
   ○ Creed   ○ homily

4. The _____ is the talk given by the priest or deacon that helps us understand the readings and the Gospel and how we are to live.
   ○ Creed   ○ homily

5. A _____ is a song of praise from the Bible.
   ○ Gospel   ○ psalm

6. We learn the Good News about Jesus' life and teachings by listening to the _____.
   ○ first reading   ○ Gospel

7–8. Who do we pray for in the Prayer of the Faithful?

_____

9–10. What do we learn by listening to God's Word at Mass?

_____

✝ We Gather in Prayer

Leader: Write your initials in each gift box to show that you offer God all that you think, say, and do.

Now stand and lift up your books. Echo each line of the prayer.

We lift our minds and hearts in prayer. (Echo)

God, we offer to you today (Echo)

All we think, and do, and say, (Echo)

Uniting it with what was done (Echo)

On earth by Jesus Christ, your Son. (Echo)

We bring forward the gifts of bread and wine.

WE GATHER

✚ *God, we offer you all that we think and do and say.*

Justin's Aunt Sara gave him an art kit for his birthday. He used the crayons from the kit to make her a thank-you card.

Why was this a good way for Justin to thank his aunt?

WE BELIEVE

The **Liturgy of the Eucharist** is the second main part of the Mass. During the Liturgy of the Eucharist we present the gifts of bread and wine. A very special prayer is prayed. The bread and wine become the Body and Blood of Christ. We receive the Body and Blood of Christ.

The Liturgy of the Eucharist begins as the priest prepares the altar. This is also the time when we give money or other gifts for the Church and the poor. Ushers or other members of the assembly collect these gifts.

As Catholics...

The Church uses a special plate and cup at Mass. The plate is called a *paten*. The paten holds the bread that will become the Body of Christ. The cup is called a *chalice*. The chalice holds the wine that will become the Blood of Christ.

The next time you are at Mass, notice the paten and chalice.

Key Word

Liturgy of the Eucharist the second main part of the Mass in which the gifts of bread and wine become the Body and Blood of Christ

Then members of the assembly bring forward the gifts of bread and wine. During this time we may sing a song. We remember that everything we have is a gift from God. We will offer these gifts and ourselves back to God.

The priest prepares these gifts of bread and wine with special prayers. We can respond: "Blessed be God for ever."

Then we are all invited to pray that the Lord will accept these gifts.

WE RESPOND

How can we show God we are thankful for his gifts?

♫ A Gift From Your Children

Here is our gift, the bread and the wine:
A symbol of sharing, a beautiful sign:
A gift, a gift from your children;
A gift, a gift of our love.

Here is our gift, the song that we sing:
Raising our voices, praising your name!
Here is our gift, the song of our heart:
A gift, a gift of our love.

The Eucharistic Prayer is the great prayer of thanks and praise.

WE GATHER

✠ *Holy, holy, holy, Lord*

What are some different ways to show your thanks to others?

WE BELIEVE

After the preparation of the gifts, we pray the most important prayer in the Mass. This prayer is called the **Eucharistic Prayer**. It is the great prayer of praise and thanksgiving. This prayer is prayed in our name by the priest.

During this prayer we pray for many things. We lift up our hearts to the Lord. We remember all the things God has done for us. We praise God by singing "Holy, holy, holy. . . ." We call on the power of the Holy Spirit. We remember what Jesus said and did at the Last Supper.

The priest takes the bread. He says the words that Jesus said at the Last Supper. "TAKE THIS, ALL OF YOU, AND EAT OF IT, FOR THIS IS MY BODY, WHICH WILL BE GIVEN UP FOR YOU."

Then the priest takes the cup of wine. He says:
"TAKE THIS, ALL OF YOU, AND DRINK FROM IT, FOR THIS IS THE CHALICE OF MY BLOOD. . . ."

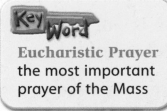

Key Word

Eucharistic Prayer
the most important prayer of the Mass

This part of the Eucharistic Prayer is called the Consecration. By the power of the Holy Spirit and through the words and actions of the priest, the bread and wine become the Body and Blood of Christ. This is called transubstantiation.

What looks like bread and tastes like bread is not bread anymore. What looks like wine and tastes like wine is not wine anymore. The bread and wine have become the Body and Blood of Christ. As Catholics we believe that Jesus Christ is really present in the Eucharist.

The priest invites us to proclaim our faith. We pray:
"When we eat this Bread and drink this Cup, we proclaim your Death, O Lord, until you come again."

We pray that the Holy Spirit will unite all those who believe in Jesus.

We end the Eucharistic Prayer by responding "Amen." When we pray this word, we are saying "Yes, I believe." We are saying "yes" to the prayer the priest has prayed in our name.

Circle the words we say when we proclaim our faith.

WE RESPOND

Talk about what happens during the Eucharistic Prayer.

How can we show that we believe in Jesus?

We pray the Our Father and ask God for forgiveness and peace.

WE GATHER

✝ *Jesus, we believe in your presence.*

> 🧍 Use your own words to write one thing we pray for when we pray the Our Father.
>
> _____
>
> _____

WE BELIEVE

After the Eucharistic Prayer, we prepare to receive the Body and Blood of Christ. We join ourselves with the whole Church. We pray aloud or sing the Our Father.

After the Our Father, the priest reminds us of Jesus' words at the Last Supper. Jesus said, "Peace I leave with you; my peace I give to you." (John 14:27) We pray that Christ's peace may be with us always. We turn to the people who are near us and offer them a sign of peace. This action shows that we are all one. We are united to Christ and to one another.

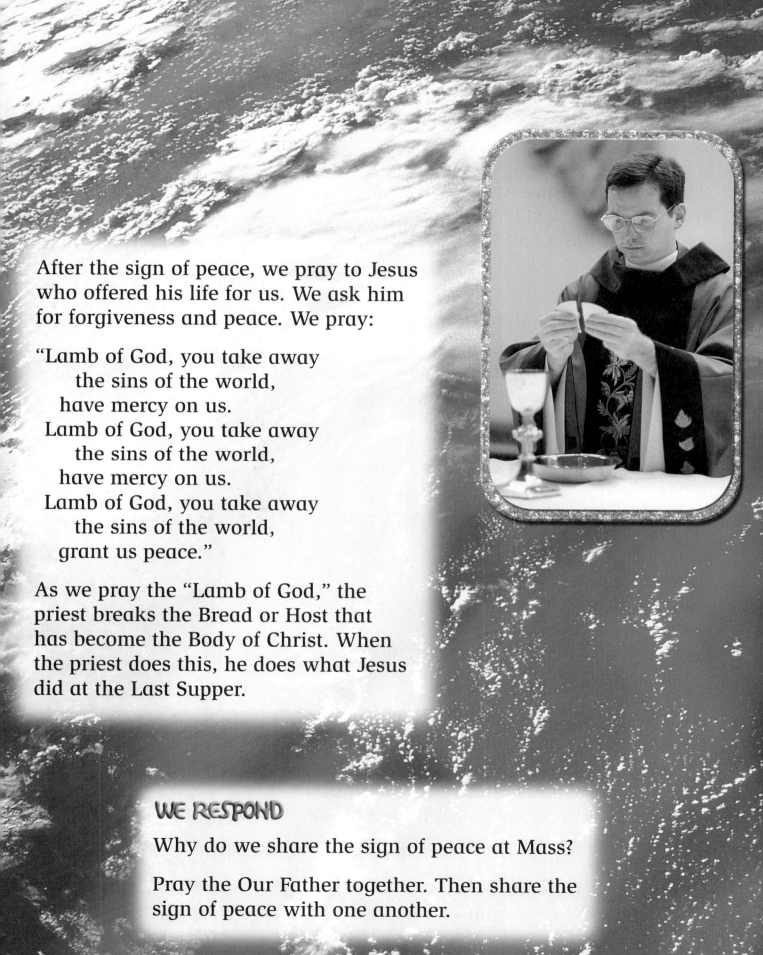

After the sign of peace, we pray to Jesus who offered his life for us. We ask him for forgiveness and peace. We pray:

"Lamb of God, you take away
    the sins of the world,
  have mercy on us.
Lamb of God, you take away
    the sins of the world,
  have mercy on us.
Lamb of God, you take away
    the sins of the world,
  grant us peace."

As we pray the "Lamb of God," the priest breaks the Bread or Host that has become the Body of Christ. When the priest does this, he does what Jesus did at the Last Supper.

WE RESPOND

Why do we share the sign of peace at Mass?

Pray the Our Father together. Then share the sign of peace with one another.

213

We receive Jesus Christ in Holy Communion.

WE GATHER

✝ *Jesus, you are the Lamb of God.*

Think about a time when you were invited to take part in an important event. How did it feel to be part of this?

WE BELIEVE

After we pray "Lamb of God," we are invited to share in the Eucharist. The priest holds up the Host that has become the Body of Christ. The priest says,
"Behold the Lamb of God,
behold him who takes away the sins of
    the world.
Blessed are those called to the supper of
    the Lamb."

We respond,
"Lord, I am not worthy that you should
    enter under my roof,
but only say the word and my soul shall
    be healed."

If we have received first Holy Communion, we go forward to receive the Body and Blood of Christ. The priest, deacon, or extraordinary minister of Holy Communion shows the Host to each person who goes forward and says,
"The Body of Christ."
Each person responds, "Amen"
and receives Holy Communion.

214

Then the priest, deacon, or extraordinary minister of Holy Communion may hand the cup to each person saying, "The Blood of Christ." Each person responds, "Amen" and drinks from the cup.

While the assembly receives Holy Communion, we all sing a song of thanksgiving. We are united with one another.

Then there is usually some quiet time. During this time we remember Jesus is present within us. We thank Jesus for the gift of himself in Holy Communion.

WE RESPOND

What can you do to thank Jesus for the gift of himself in the Eucharist?

🎵 Jesus, You Are Bread for Us

Jesus, you are bread for us.
Jesus, you are life for us.
In your gift of Eucharist
  we find love.

When we feel we need a friend,
  you are there with us, Jesus.
Thank you for the friend you are.
Thank you for the love we share.

PROJECT

Show What *you* Know

Circle the Key Word that names the second main part of the Mass in which the gifts of bread and wine become the Body and Blood of Christ.

Underline the Key Word that names the most important prayer of the Mass.

> Liturgy of the Eucharist   Eucharistic Prayer

Celebrate!

Put the parts of the Liturgy of the Eucharist in order. The first one has been done for you.

☐	Sign of peace
1	Presentation of gifts
☐	Our Father
☐	Lamb of God
☐	Holy Communion
☐	Eucharistic Prayer

DISCIPLE

Pray
Learn
Celebrate
Share
Choose
Live

Picture This

Look at the photo. What important prayer is the priest praying in our name?

_____

_____

Make *it* Happen

In some parishes, people volunteer to be prayer partners with those preparing for their first Holy Communion. In the space below, write a prayer for prayer partners to pray together.

↳**DISCIPLE CHALLENGE** Pray your prayer for those receiving first Holy Communion in your parish.

Take Home

Discuss with your family why it is an honor to bring forward the gifts at Mass. Write your thoughts here.

_____

_____

_____

_____

CHAPTER TEST

Fill in the circle beside the correct answer.

1. The second main part of the Mass is the _____.
   ○ Our Father   ○ Liturgy of the Eucharist

2. Bread and wine become the Body and Blood of Christ during the _____.
   ○ Our Father   ○ Eucharistic Prayer

3. When we pray "Amen," we are saying _____.
   ○ have mercy   ○ Yes, I believe

4. Right after we pray the _____, we are invited to share in the Eucharist.
   ○ Lamb of God   ○ Creed

Order these actions of the Liturgy of the Eucharist, 1 to 4.

5. We offer each other a sign of peace.   _____

6. We receive Holy Communion.   _____

7. We bring forward gifts of bread and wine.   _____

8. The Eucharistic Prayer begins.   _____

9–10. Why is the Eucharistic Prayer the most important prayer of the Mass?

✝ We Gather in Prayer

Leader: Let us listen to what Jesus told his disciples at the Last Supper.

Reader: Jesus said, "As I have loved you, so you also should love one another. This is how all will know that you are my disciples, if you have love for one another." (John 13:34–35)

Group 1: When we show respect for all people,

All: Jesus, we do as you asked.

Group 2: When we are kind and helpful,

All: Jesus, we do as you asked.

Group 3: When we forgive others,

All: Jesus, we do as you asked.

All: Jesus, help us to share your love and peace with others.

Amen.

We are sent to share God's love with others.

WE GATHER

✝ *Jesus, may we follow your loving ways.*

🧍 What happens in your classroom at the end of your school day? Show what you say and do.

WE BELIEVE

The first disciples were sent out to continue Jesus' work. We are also disciples. Jesus asks us to continue his work, too.

The word *Mass* comes from a word that means "sending out." At the end of every Mass, the priest sends us out to share God's love with others.

Before we are sent out, the priest blesses us. We make the Sign of the Cross as he says,

"May almighty God bless you, the Father, and the Son, † and the Holy Spirit."

We respond, "Amen."

Then the deacon or priest sends us to share God's love with others. He may say, "Go in peace."

We respond, "Thanks be to God."

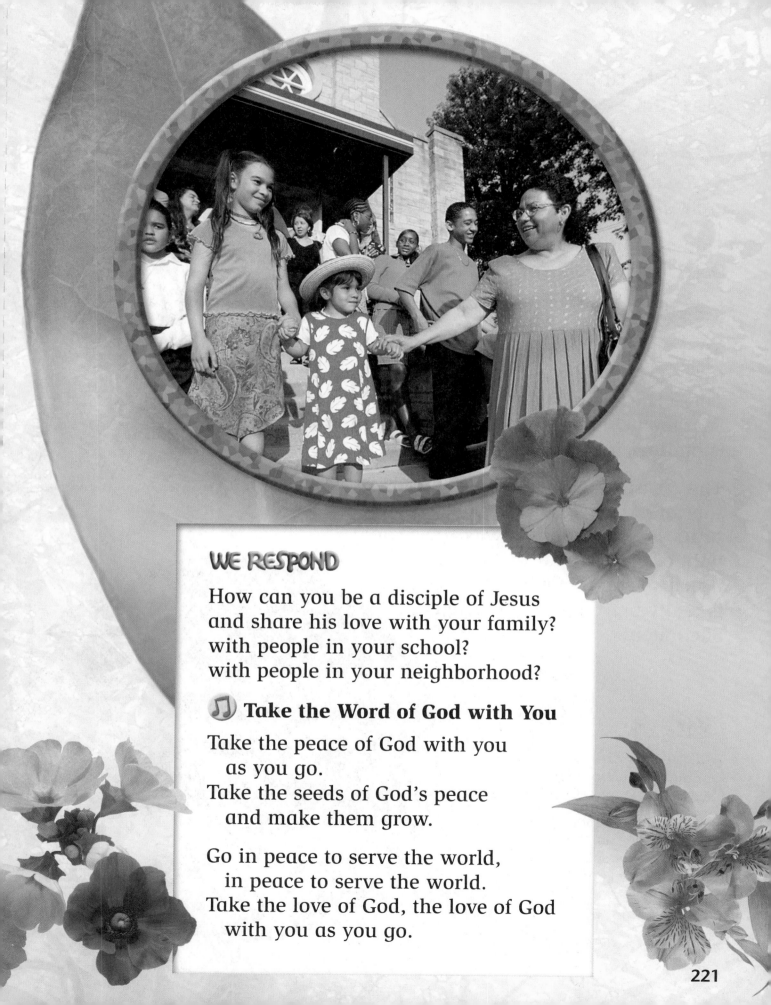

WE RESPOND

How can you be a disciple of Jesus
and share his love with your family?
with people in your school?
with people in your neighborhood?

♫ Take the Word of God with You

Take the peace of God with you
　　as you go.
Take the seeds of God's peace
　　and make them grow.

Go in peace to serve the world,
　　in peace to serve the world.
Take the love of God, the love of God
　　with you as you go.

Jesus is present in the Blessed Sacrament.

WE GATHER

✝ *Jesus help us to remember that you are with us always.*

Think about the church in your parish. Describe the inside of the church.

WE BELIEVE

After Holy Communion there may be Hosts that have not been received. These Hosts are called the Blessed Sacrament. The **Blessed Sacrament** is another name for the Eucharist.

The Blessed Sacrament is kept in the special place in the church called the **tabernacle**. There is always a special light or candle near the tabernacle. It helps us to remember that Jesus is really present in the Blessed Sacrament.

Blessed Sacrament another name for the Eucharist

tabernacle the special place in the church in which the Blessed Sacrament is kept

After Mass and at other times, priests, deacons, and extraordinary ministers of Holy Communion take the Blessed Sacrament from the tabernacle. They bring the Blessed Sacrament as Holy Communion to those who are sick and to those who are not able to join the parish community for Mass. The Blessed Sacrament strengthens all those who receive it.

WE RESPOND

Jesus wants us to share God's love with those who are sick. We can do this by praying for them. We can also do this by visiting them or sending them get-well messages.

Design a card for someone who is sick. Tell them you are praying for them.

Jesus is with the Church as we share God's love.

WE GATHER

✝ *Jesus, help us to love and serve others as you did.*

Think about your good friends. How do other people know you are good friends?

WE BELIEVE

The early Christians were friends and followers of Jesus. They celebrated the Eucharist often. Receiving Jesus in the Eucharist helped their community. They were united with Jesus and one another. They were able to share God's love with others.

The early Christians learned and prayed together. They shared what they had with those who were poor and hungry. They tried to help those who were sad or lonely.

When people looked at the way the early Christians lived, they wanted to live as the Christians did. They wanted to become a part of Jesus' community, the Church.

Please give

When we receive Jesus in Holy Communion, our friendship with him grows. Receiving Holy Communion helps us to love God and others. It helps us to be followers of Jesus. It helps us to be part of our parish. Together we show others what God's love is like.

Match the ways we can follow the example of the early Christians.

What the early Christians did	What we can do today
They fed those who were hungry. •	• We try to be calm and kind at home and in school.
They tried to live in peace with their families and others. •	• We pray with others. We take part in the Mass and celebrate the other sacraments.
They praised and thanked God often. •	• We collect food and clothing to give to those in need.

WE RESPOND

Who shows you what God's love is like? How?

What can you do together to share God's love in your parish? in your neighborhood?

Jesus is with us as we share his peace with others.

WE GATHER

✝ *Jesus, may we follow your peaceful ways.*

Look at the picture. What happens when you drop a pebble in water?

WE BELIEVE

During Mass we ask Jesus to give us peace. At the end of Mass, the deacon or priest tells us, "Go in peace." Jesus wants us to share his peace with others.

Every time we make a choice to be peaceful, we are like pebbles dropped in water. We spread Jesus' love and peace throughout the world.

WE RESPOND

Ⓧ Read the following stories. Draw a 💧 beside the peaceful choice.

• Mia and Carlos had a fight yesterday.

____ Mia thought, "I'm never going to talk to Carlos again."

____ Mia called Carlos. She said, "I'm sorry."

- Mrs. Pulski told the class, "We are going to learn about people in other countries. This may help us to live in peace with them."

_____ Joseph thought, "Why do I have to learn about other countries? I don't care about people who live far away."

_____ Joseph learned about the people of other lands. He shared what he learned with his family and friends.

- Cara's brother and sister are angry with each other.

_____ Cara told her brother that their sister said something mean about him.

_____ Cara told her brother and sister that they should make up with each other.

What are other ways to share Jesus' peace with others?

Pray these words quietly. When you see ◌, think about what you can do to share the peace of Jesus Christ.

Jesus, help us make peaceful choices. Help us to spread your peace and love

- in our homes ◌

- in our neighborhood ◌

- in our city or town ◌

- in the world ◌.

PROJECT

Show What you Know

tabernacle

Blessed Sacrament

Write the two Key Words in one sentence.

_____

_____ .

What Would you do?

Imagine that you could write a recipe for being a disciple. What are some ingredients it might include?

1 cup of God's love

1 cup of _____

1 cup of _____

½ cup of _____

1 teaspoon of _____

DISCIPLE

Pray
Learn
Celebrate
Share
Choose
Live

Make *it* Happen

Write a story about an early Christian who was a friend and follower of Jesus. Then, share the story with your classmates and family. Talk about ways this early Christian is like a disciple today.

Take Home

Make a list of things that make family life more peaceful.

_____

_____

_____

As a family, talk about your list.

↳ **DISCIPLE CHALLENGE** Decide on one thing you all can do this week to make your home more peaceful.

CHAPTER TEST

Circle the correct answer.

1. Does the word *Mass* come from a word that means "giving thanks"?   **Yes**   **No**

2. Is Jesus present in the Blessed Sacrament?   **Yes**   **No**

3. Is the tabernacle the special place in the church in which the Blessed Sacrament is kept?   **Yes**   **No**

4. Did the early Christians celebrate the Eucharist only a few times a year?   **Yes**   **No**

5–6. Write two things that happen at the end of Mass.

_____

_____

7–8. Write two ways the early Christians shared God's love.

_____

_____

9–10. Write two ways receiving Holy Communion helps us.

_____

_____

"Turn away from sin and be faithful to the gospel."

The Marking of Ashes

SEASONAL

CHAPTER 20

This chapter offers preparation for the season of Lent.

Lent is a season of preparing.

WE GATHER

Sometimes a special logo or mark stands for something or someone. Think about some logos or marks that you know. What do they stand for?

WE BELIEVE

Lent is a time of remembering all that Jesus did to save us. It is a time to get ready. We get ready for the celebration of Easter and the new life that Jesus brings us.

The season of Lent lasts forty days. During that time we pray to God and ask for his forgiveness. We thank him for his mercy.

Lent begins on a day called Ash Wednesday. On Ash Wednesday, Catholics are marked with blessed ashes. The ashes are used to make a cross on our foreheads.

The cross reminds us that Jesus suffered and died for each of us. He did this so that we could live with God forever.

The cross of ashes on our foreheads is a sign that we are sorry for our sins and want to follow Jesus.

Lent is a time when we try to grow closer to Jesus. We follow Jesus by praying, doing good things for others, and helping the poor. We treat people with love and respect, the way Jesus did.

Look at the photos on this page.

Talk about the ways people are following Jesus.

WE RESPOND

The color of the season of Lent is violet or purple. On the chart, color the word *Lent*. During Lent, each time you show your love for God and others, draw a cross in one of these boxes.

LENT

✚ We Respond in Prayer

Leader: Loving God, open our ears and our hearts to the message of your Son.

Reader: A reading from the Gospel of Luke.

"Or what woman having ten coins and losing one would not light a lamp and sweep the house, searching carefully until she finds it? And when she does find it, she calls together her friends and neighbors and says to them, 'Rejoice with me because I have found the coin that I lost.' In just the same way, I tell you, there will be rejoicing among the angels of God over one sinner who repents." (Luke 15:8–10)

The Gospel of the Lord.

All: Praise to you, Lord Jesus Christ.

 **We Are Yours, O Lord**

Help us to remember
who and what we are:
We are yours, O Lord.

Pray
Learn
Celebrate
Share
Choose
Live

Grade 2 Lent

PROJECT DISCIPLE

Picture This
Complete the chart about Lent.
Use words or pictures.

The color of Lent is	Lent begins on	A sign of Lent is	The number of days in Lent

Celebrate!

Connect the dots to find a sign of Lent.
Then, color it in.

1●   ●2

13●   14●   ●3   ●4

12●   11●   ●6   ●5

10●   ●7

9●   ●8

Take Home

Think of a person who needs your prayer during Lent. Write his or her name in this prayer.

Let the light of God shine on

_____.

Say your prayer together.

↳ **DISCIPLE CHALLENGE**
Talk about what you can do during the season to help this person.

"We should glory in the cross of our Lord Jesus Christ."

Evening Mass of the Lord's Supper

SEASONAL

CHAPTER 21

This chapter includes the three days from Holy Thursday evening until Easter Sunday.

The Three Days celebrate the Death and Resurrection of Jesus.

WE GATHER

Have you ever been to a celebration that lasted more than one day? What was it?

WE BELIEVE

During Lent we prepare to celebrate Jesus' Death and Resurrection in a special way. When Lent ends, we begin the Three Days.

The Three Days are the Church's greatest celebration. They are the most important days of the Church year. During the Three Days, called the Easter Triduum, we gather with our parish. We gather to celebrate at night and during the day. The Easter Triduum begins on Holy Thursday evening and ends on Easter Sunday evening.

Trace over the lines to show when the Three Days begin and end.

DAY 1   **DAY 2**   **DAY 3**

| Holy Thursday | Good Friday | Holy Saturday | Easter Sunday |

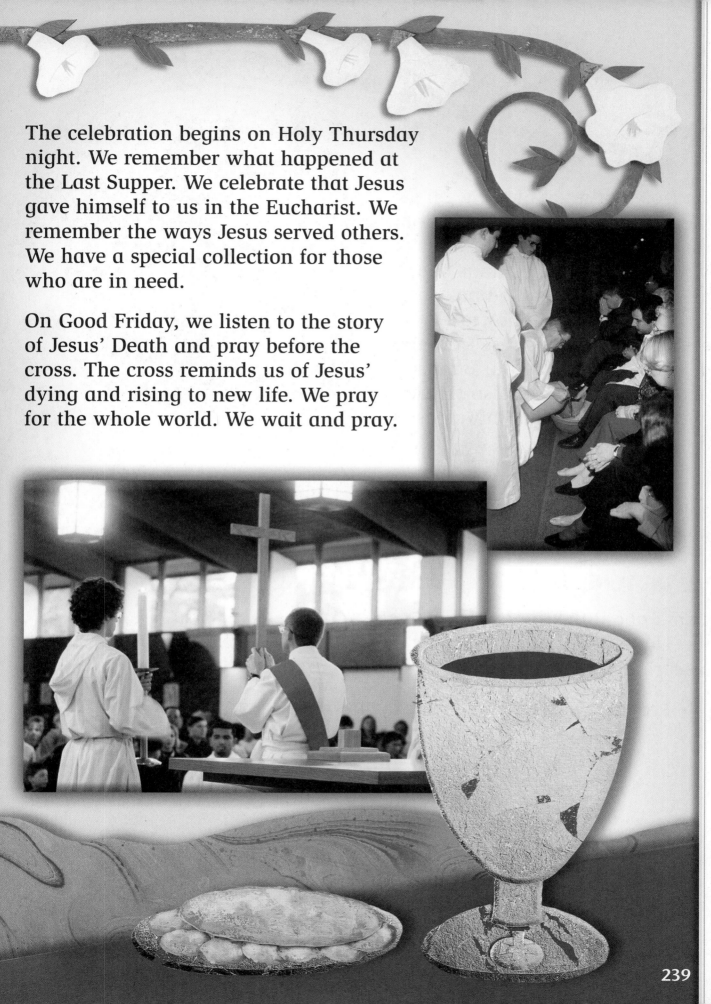

The celebration begins on Holy Thursday night. We remember what happened at the Last Supper. We celebrate that Jesus gave himself to us in the Eucharist. We remember the ways Jesus served others. We have a special collection for those who are in need.

On Good Friday, we listen to the story of Jesus' Death and pray before the cross. The cross reminds us of Jesus' dying and rising to new life. We pray for the whole world. We wait and pray.

On Holy Saturday night, we light the Easter candle. Jesus has risen! He brings light to the darkness. We listen to Bible readings about all the great things God has done for us. We sing with joy to celebrate that Jesus rose from the dead. We remember our Baptism in a special way. We also welcome new members of the Church as they are baptized.

Holy Saturday turns into Easter Sunday. We sing songs of joy and praise as we begin the Easter season. Alleluia!

WE RESPOND

Think about the things we do to celebrate the Three Days. How does your parish celebrate the Three Days?

Pray this prayer. Then color the frame.

When we eat this Bread and drink this Cup,
we proclaim your Death, O Lord,
until you come again.

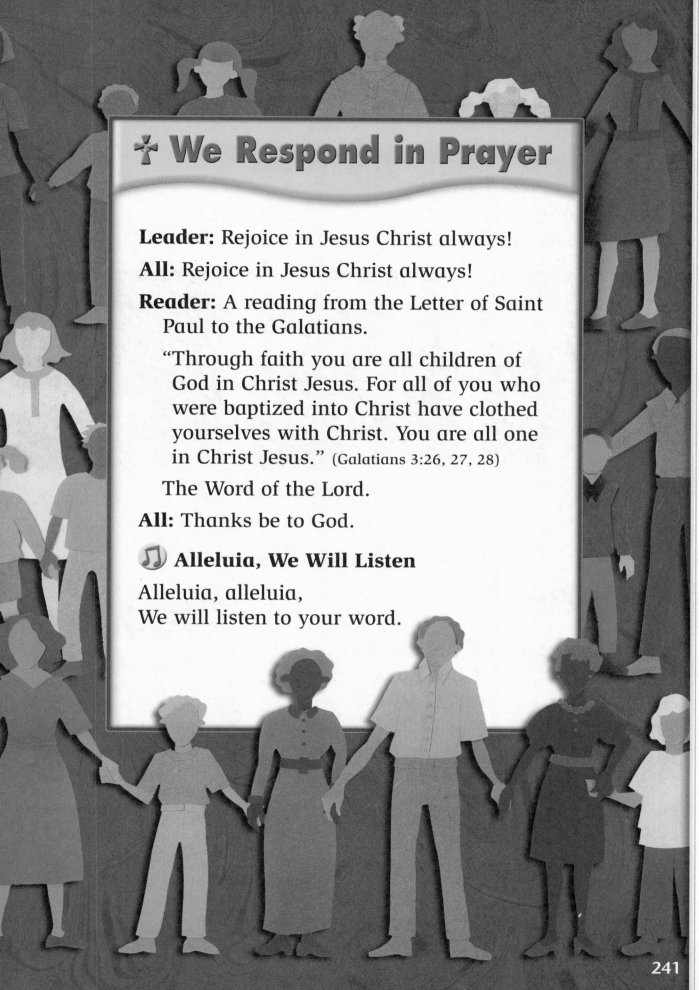

✞ We Respond in Prayer

Leader: Rejoice in Jesus Christ always!

All: Rejoice in Jesus Christ always!

Reader: A reading from the Letter of Saint Paul to the Galatians.

"Through faith you are all children of God in Christ Jesus. For all of you who were baptized into Christ have clothed yourselves with Christ. You are all one in Christ Jesus." (Galatians 3:26, 27, 28)

The Word of the Lord.

All: Thanks be to God.

🎵 **Alleluia, We Will Listen**

Alleluia, alleluia,
We will listen to your word.

Show What *you* Know

Put these events in the order that they are celebrated during the Three Days.

_____ _____ _____

Celebrate!

Draw a picture of one way that you will celebrate during the Three Days.

Take Home

Now that the above pictures are in order, use them to talk about the Three Days. Touch each picture as you tell your family why it is important.

Use the words in the box to complete the sentences.

1. In the Eucharist we remember and

   _____ what Jesus
   did at the Last Supper.

2. The word *eucharist* means

   _____.

3. We receive the Body and Blood of

   Christ in _____.

4. The _____ is the most important
   prayer of the Mass.

5. The _____ is a prayer in which we say
   what we believe as Christians.

6. The community of people who join together for the celebration

   of the Mass is the _____.

giving thanks

celebrate

Creed

assembly

Holy Communion

Eucharistic Prayer

continued on next page   **243**

7–8. Draw or write about two things that happen during the Liturgy of the Word.

9–10. Draw or write about two things that happen during the Liturgy of the Eucharist.

Peace and Reconciliation

Part 1 I Open My Heart

Some people find peace in nature.
Look at the picture.
Do you find it peaceful?

Draw a place where you find peace.

Share your drawing with the group.

Jesus shared peace. Jesus healed people and forgave their sins. He told them to "go in peace" (Mark 5:34).

Jesus also taught people to be peaceful and kind toward one another. He said:

"Blessed are the peacemakers,
  for they will be called children of God." (Matthew 5:9)

Peace and Reconciliation

Part 2 We Come Together for Prayer

Reader 1: While Jesus was dining with the disciples, a woman came into the room. She knelt at Jesus' feet and cried. She was sorry for her sins and asked for Jesus' forgiveness. (Based on Luke 7:36–38)

Reader 2: Jesus said to the woman, "Your faith has saved you; go in peace" (Luke 7:50).

All: Jesus, you are loving and forgiving, and you give us peace.

Leader: Lord Jesus, you said to your disciples, "Peace I leave with you; my peace I give to you" (John 14:27). You also taught your disciples, "Into whatever house you enter, first say, 'Peace to this household'" (Luke 10:5).

All: We thank you for giving us your peace. Help us to share your peace with others. (*All name ways they can share peace with others.*)

Leader: Let us now pray in the words of your followers who proclaimed:

All: "Blessed is the king who comes in the name of the Lord. Peace in heaven and glory in the highest." (Luke 19:38) Amen.

Catholic Identity Retreat

Peace and Reconciliation

Part 3 I Cherish God's Word

Peter asked, "'Lord, if my brother sins against me, how often must I forgive him? As many as seven times?' Jesus answered, 'I say to you, not seven times but seventy-seven times'" (Matthew 18:21–22).

READ the quotation from Scripture. Read slowly. Pay close attention to what you are reading.

REFLECT on what you read. Think about:

- Jesus always forgives us. What does he teach us about how to forgive others?

- Ask Jesus for forgiveness and peace.

- What is a time when you forgave another person, as Jesus taught?

SHARE your thoughts and feelings with God in prayer. Speak to God as a friend.

CONTEMPLATE, or sit quietly and think about God's Word in the Scripture passage from the Gospel of Matthew above.

Peace and Reconciliation

Part 4 I Value My Catholic Faith

The Gospels tell many stories about Jesus forgiving and healing people. Jesus helped people know God's mercy. He helped them experience peace. This picture shows a time when Jesus healed someone and forgave his sins.

Listen to the Scripture story. It is based on Mark 10:46–52. Talk about the story with your group. Then role-play the story together. Imagine what the man might say and feel. How did Jesus bring the man peace?

 Mark 10:46–52

A blind man sat by the roadside. The man was poor and troubled. Jesus walked by. The man cried out, "Jesus, have pity on me!"

Jesus said, "What do you want me to do for you?"

The blind man said, "Master, I want to see."

Jesus told him, "Go on your way. Your faith has saved you."

Immediately the blind man began to see! He then followed Jesus on the way.

(Based on Mark 10:46–47, 51–52)

Catholic Identity Retreat

Peace and Reconciliation

Part 5 I Celebrate Catholic Identity

Jesus calls us to forgiveness and peace. He wants us to be reconciled, or joined together again, with God and one another. As Catholics we receive the Sacrament of Penance and Reconciliation for the forgiveness of our sins. This sacrament reconciles us with God and the Church. We are given peace.

Think about ways that you, your friends, family members, or classmates share peace and reconciliation. Choose one way. Draw it on the prayer card below. Then write a prayer for peace next to it. You will pray this prayer in Part 6.

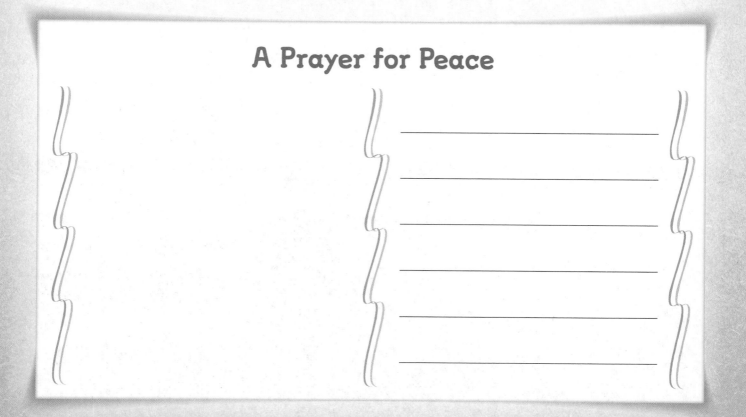

A Prayer for Peace

Peace and Reconciliation

Part 6 I Honor My Catholic Identity

Reader 1: "Return to the LORD, your God.
For gracious and merciful is he,
slow to anger, rich in kindness." (Joel 2:13)

Leader: Let us pray. Lord, you are our loving Savior. Help us to always seek your peace. Teach us to forgive others as you forgive us. Help us to get along peacefully with others.

Reader 2: Jesus said, "When you stand to pray, forgive anyone against whom you have a [disagreement]" (Mark 11:25).

Leader: Be still. Think about today. Have you asked God for forgiveness? Have you forgiven others? Think about tomorrow. How can you be more peaceful and forgiving? Ask the Holy Spirit to help you.

All: (*Take turns praying the prayer you wrote in Part 5.*)
Jesus, help us to be peacemakers.
Amen.

Catholic Identity Retreat

Bringing the Retreat Home

Peace and Reconciliation

Retreat Recap

Review the pages of your child's *Celebrating Catholic Identity: Morality* retreat. Ask your child to tell you about the retreat. Talk about peace and reconciliation:

- Jesus shared peace and reconciliation.
- Jesus offers us peace and forgiveness of sin especially through the Sacrament of Penance and Reconciliation. This sacrament reconciles us with God and the Church.
- Jesus calls us to be peaceful and forgiving people.

A Path to Peace

Using the following image or one you have drawn together, write along the path three ways to build up peace in your household. You might wish to display your completed "path to peace" where your family can view it as a reminder to be peacemakers.

Take a Moment
Think of an outdoor location that your family finds peaceful, such as a local garden, beach, or park. Spend time with your child focusing on God's creation and the feeling of peace. Pray together for peace and reconciliation in your lives, the community, and the world.

1. _____

2. _____

3. _____

Family Prayer

Saint Francis of Assisi, who lived from about 1181 to 1226, was known as a peacemaker. Pray together using his words:

Lord, make me an instrument of your peace:
where there is hatred, let me sow love;
where there is injury, pardon;
where there is doubt, faith;
where there is despair, hope;
where there is darkness, light;
where there is sadness, joy.
(Prayer of Saint Francis of Assisi)

For more resources, see the *Catholic Identity Home Companion* at the end of this book.

Why We Believe
As a Catholic Family

What if someone asks us:

- What is the Church's position on war?

The following resources can help us to respond:

As Catholics, we are opposed to unjust war and believe we must do everything possible to avoid it. We must honor the Fifth Commandment, "You shall not kill" (Exodus 20:13). The Church teaches that several conditions must be carefully and seriously considered before there is any prospect of war. These are known as the conditions for a "just war." A war can be considered just only if it meets the following conditions all at once: (1) an aggressor is damaging a nation, or community of nations, in a lasting, grave, and certain way; (2) all other means of ending the conflict have been tried and failed; (3) the war has serious prospects of success; and (4) the war will not cause greater destruction and evil than the aggression it was meant to stop. (See *CCC*, 2309.)

The Church asks all government leaders and citizens to avoid war by seeking peaceful and just ends to hatred and conflicts.

🌿 What does Scripture say?

"Blessed are the peacemakers,
   for they will be called children of God."
(Matthew 5:9)

"You have heard that it was said, 'You shall love your neighbor and hate your enemy.' But I say to you, love your enemies, and pray for those who persecute you."
(Matthew 5:43–44)

"Let us then pursue what leads to peace and to building up one another." (Romans 14:19)

The Church continues to proclaim Jesus' message of peace and, in her social teachings, addresses the

causes of conflict as well. The Church encourages peace—in our families, among neighbors, and among nations.

As Catholics we must work for peace and justice by being peacemakers in our own daily lives. The Church calls us to pray for an end to wars and to address the root causes of war, insofar as we are able.

🌿 What does the Church say?

"Because of the evils and injustices that all war brings with it, we must do everything reasonably possible to avoid it. The Church prays: 'From famine, pestilence, and war, O Lord, deliver us.'" (*CCC*, 2327)

"I make a forceful and urgent call to the entire Catholic Church, . . . to every Christian of other confessions, . . . to followers of every religion and to those brothers and sisters who do not believe: peace is a good which overcomes every barrier, because it belongs to all of humanity!"
(Pope Francis, Angelus message, September 1, 2013)

"Who is there who does not feel the craving to be rid of the threat of war, and to see peace preserved and made daily more secure?" (Saint John XXIII, *Pacem in Terris* ("Peace on Earth"), 115)

Notes:

We Live Our Catholic Faith

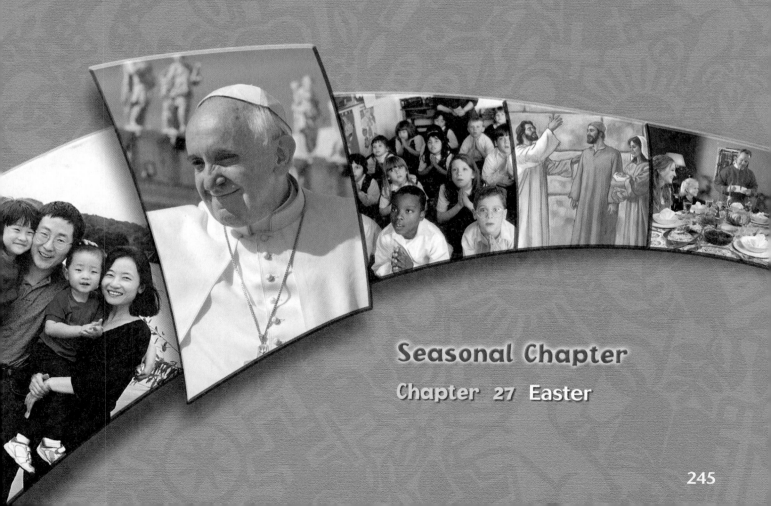

Seasonal Chapter

PROJECT DISCIPLE
DEAR FAMILY

In Unit 4 your child will grow as a disciple of Jesus by:

- learning about the ways people can serve God as married or single people, ordained men, and religious
- praying, celebrating at Mass and the sacraments, and with our parish community caring for those in need
- learning about the ways the pope and the bishops lead and serve the Church
- talking and listening to God in prayer
- honoring Mary and the saints by following their example of discipleship.

Saint Stories

Some popes and bishops who served the Church have been named saints. Saint Pius X was the pope from 1903–1914. As Pope, he wanted to ensure that children received their first Holy Communion at an early age. He is the patron saint of first communicants.

Saint Charles Borromeo was the Archbishop of Milan, Italy. Saint Charles began Sunday school for children, showed great care for the sick, and served his diocese with great love. He is the patron saint of bishops.

Share these saint stories with your child. Ask these two saints to help our pope and bishops.

Pray Today

Chapter 22 presents the different vocations to which God calls people. Pray together:

God, you call each of us to serve you.
Bless your people:
single and married,
priests and deacons,
brothers and sisters.
Help each of us to answer your call
and to serve you with love. Amen.

Reality Check

"The *Christian family* is the first place of education in prayer."
(*Catechism of the Catholic Church*, 2685)

Fast Facts

The Mass is celebrated in many languages throughout the United States, according to the native language of the people who are gathered. Mass is also celebrated in the Latin language, which was until the mid-1960s the only language used for Mass in most countries.

Show That You Care

In Chapter 26, your child will learn about God's many gifts to us—including the gift of creation. Talk about the ways your family cares for creation. Decide on one extra thing you all can do to care for the environment this week.

Take Home

Each chapter in your child's *We Believe* Grade 2 text offers a "Take Home" activity that invites your family to support your child's journey to more fully become a disciple of Christ.

Be ready for this unit's Take Home:

Chapter 22: Discussing your child's vocation

Chapter 23: Sharing family faith traditions

Chapter 24: Praying an evening prayer

Chapter 25: Finding works of art depicting Mary

Chapter 26: Being a disciple of Jesus Christ

God Calls Us to Love and Serve

22

✝ We Gather in Prayer

Leader: God, our Father, in Baptism you called us by name making us members of your people, the Church.

All: We praise you for your goodness. We thank you for your gifts.

Leader: We ask you to strengthen us to live in love and service to others as your Son, Jesus, did.

We ask this through Christ, our Lord.

All: Amen.

We are called by God.

WE GATHER

✝ *God, help us to show others your love.*

Think about a time when your parent called your name. What did you do when you heard your name called?

WE BELIEVE

We read in the Bible that God says, "I have called you by name: you are mine." (Isaiah 43:1)

When we are **called by God**, we are invited by God to love and serve him.

We love and serve God now in many ways. We do and say things to show our love for God.

As members of the Church we pray and respect God's name. We take part in the Mass and celebrate the other sacraments. We learn about God from the teachings of Jesus and the Church. We tell others the wonderful things God has done for us. These are some of the ways we love and serve God.

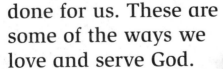

As we grow older we are called to serve God in different ways. We may serve God as single or married people, religious brothers or sisters, or priests or deacons. These ways of serving God are all important to the Church. Together we work to bring God's love to others.

called by God invited by God to love and serve him

WE RESPOND

Complete the following chart.

People who serve God	What they do

What is one thing you can do to love and serve God this week?

Married people and single people are called by God.

WE GATHER

✝ *Jesus, show us the way to love one another.*

 Family members have many ways to show love for one another. Make up a storyboard about a loving family.

WE BELIEVE

In our families there are single people and married people. They serve God in many of the same ways.

- They love and care for their families.

- They take part in parish activities.

- They tell others about Jesus and the Church.

- They work to make their communities better places.

Single people and married people also serve God by helping people who are in need. They spend time with people who are lonely. They visit people who are sick. They pray for others.

Single people serve God by serving others. They share God's love in their families, communities, and the Church.

Married people celebrate the Sacrament of Matrimony. A husband and wife share God's love in special ways with each other and with their children. They teach their children about Jesus and the Church. They show them how to live as Catholics.

WE RESPOND

Tell about ways families can show love for God and others.

🎵 God Has Made Us a Family

Chorus
God has made us a family
   and together we will grow in love.
God has made us a family
   and together we will grow in love.

Oh! Yes! We need one another,
   as together we grow in love;
and we will forgive one another,
   as together we grow in love. (Chorus)

Priests are called by God.

WE GATHER

✝ *God, thank you for your love.*

Name the priests who work in your parish.

WE BELIEVE

Some men are called, or invited, to serve God and the Church as priests. A man becomes a priest when he receives the Sacrament of Holy Orders.

Priests spend their lives sharing God's love with people. Priests share the message of Jesus. They help us to live as Jesus did.

Priests lead the celebration of the Mass and other sacraments. They teach us about our Catholic faith. They work in parishes, schools, hospitals, and communities all over the world.

As Catholics...

Deacons are baptized men who have received the Sacrament of Holy Orders. Some men are deacons for life, or permanent deacons. These men may be married or single. Other men become deacons as a step before they become priests.

Deacons serve the Church by assisting the bishops and priests. Deacons serve in their parishes by baptizing new members into the Church and by witnessing at marriages. They can proclaim the Gospel and give the homily at Mass. Deacons also have a special responsibility to serve people in need.

Is there a deacon serving in your parish?

WE RESPOND

Look at the pictures on these pages. How is each priest loving and serving God and others?

 Draw a thank-you card for your parish priest. Thank him for all he does for God and others.

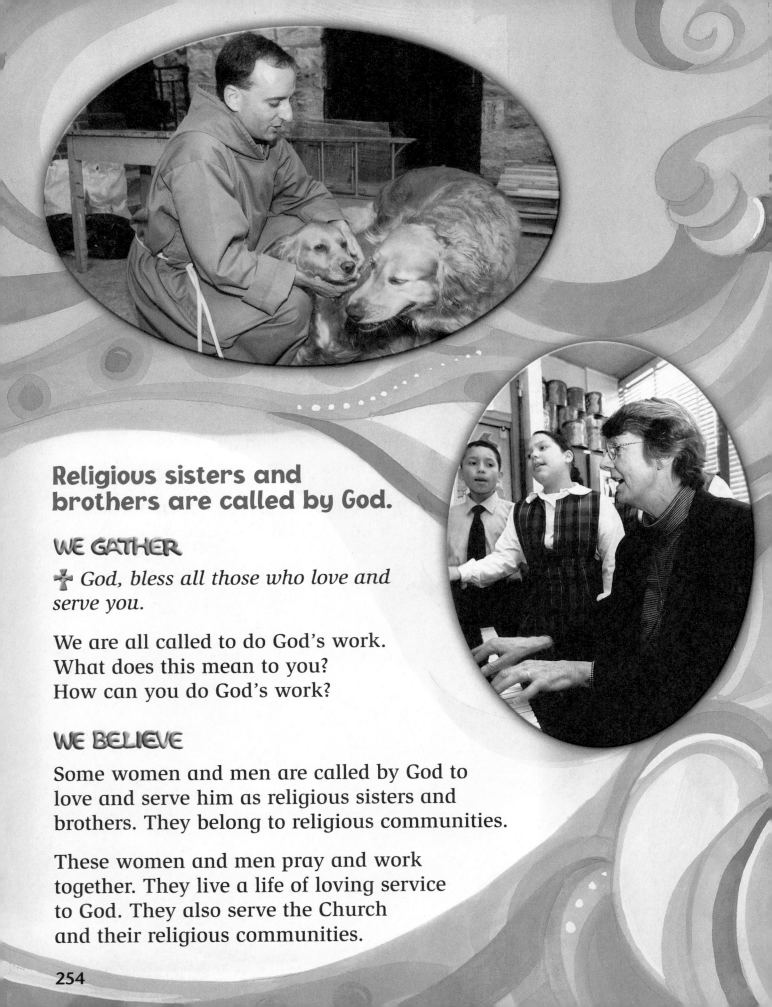

Religious sisters and brothers are called by God.

WE GATHER

✝ *God, bless all those who love and serve you.*

We are all called to do God's work. What does this mean to you? How can you do God's work?

WE BELIEVE

Some women and men are called by God to love and serve him as religious sisters and brothers. They belong to religious communities.

These women and men pray and work together. They live a life of loving service to God. They also serve the Church and their religious communities.

254

Religious sisters and brothers spend their lives sharing God's love with people. They serve in many ways.

- They can tell others about Jesus either in our country or in faraway places.

- They can teach in schools and parishes.

- They can work in hospitals and spend time with those who are sick or elderly.

- They can care for people who are poor or in need.

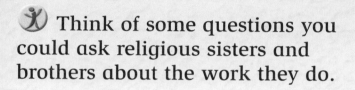 Think of some questions you could ask religious sisters and brothers about the work they do.

Write your questions here.

_____

_____

_____

_____

WE RESPOND

Why do you think some men and women choose to live their lives as religious brothers or sisters?

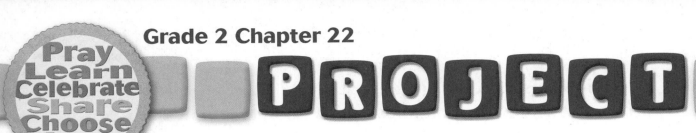

PROJECT

Show What *you* Know

Complete the web to show who is called by God. Use the chapter's faith statements to help you.

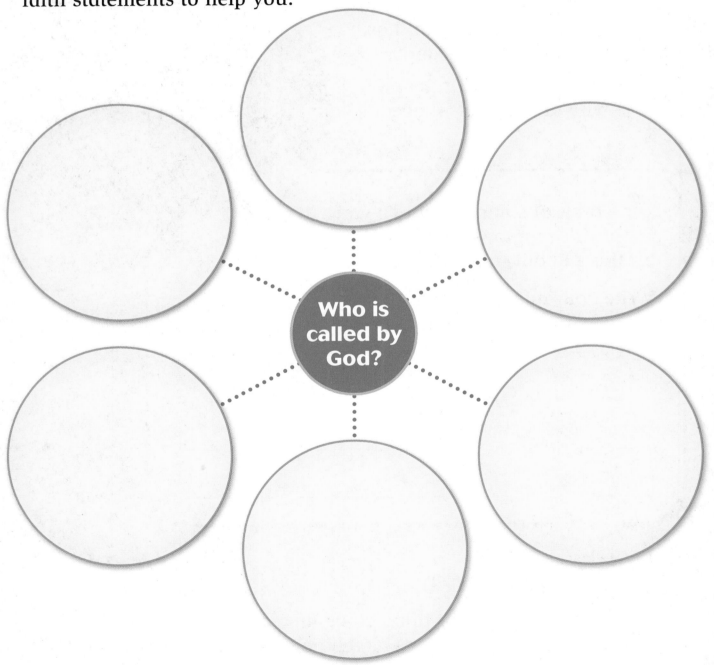

Who is called by God?

DISCIPLE

Pray
Learn
Celebrate
Share
Choose
Live

Make it Happen

Complete this trading card about a person you know who serves God.

Name:

_____

Shows love for God and others by:

_____

Saint Stories

Elizabeth Ann Seton is the first person from the United States to be named a saint. She taught and helped the poor. She started the first Catholic school in the United States. She started a religious community called the Sisters of Charity. They teach in schools, work in hospitals, and help in parishes today.

Take Home

Talk with your family about the person you want to be when you grow up. Make a list of ways that you will show your love for God when you are a grown-up.

_____

_____

_____

_____

257

CHAPTER TEST

Circle the correct answer.

1. Does God call all the members of the Church to love and serve him? **Yes   No**

2. Does a man become a priest when he celebrates the Sacrament of Matrimony? **Yes   No**

3. Do married people and single people serve God in many of the same ways? **Yes   No**

4. Are only women called to serve God in religious communities? **Yes   No**

Check the ways you are called to love and serve God.

5. _____ Respect God's name.

6. _____ Learn about God from the teachings of Jesus and the Church.

7. _____ Not share all the wonderful things God has done for us.

Write one way each of the following groups is called to love and serve God.

8. Married people _____

9. Religious brothers and sisters _____

10. Priests _____

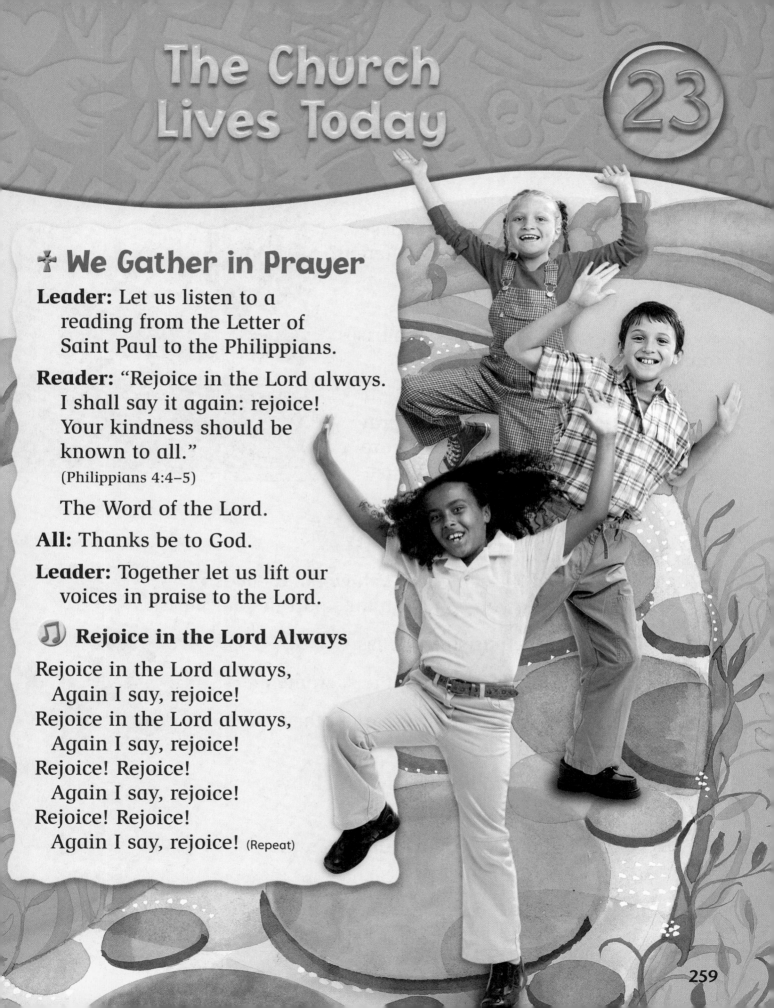

The Church Lives Today

✝ We Gather in Prayer

Leader: Let us listen to a reading from the Letter of Saint Paul to the Philippians.

Reader: "Rejoice in the Lord always. I shall say it again: rejoice! Your kindness should be known to all."
(Philippians 4:4–5)

The Word of the Lord.

All: Thanks be to God.

Leader: Together let us lift our voices in praise to the Lord.

🎵 Rejoice in the Lord Always

Rejoice in the Lord always,
  Again I say, rejoice!
Rejoice in the Lord always,
  Again I say, rejoice!
Rejoice! Rejoice!
  Again I say, rejoice!
Rejoice! Rejoice!
  Again I say, rejoice! (Repeat)

Catholics belong to parish communities.

WE GATHER

✝ *God, help us as we try to do your work.*

You belong to a family. You also belong to your class at school. How are these groups the same? How are they different?

WE BELIEVE

As Catholics we also belong to a parish family. A parish is a community of Catholics who worship and work together.

As a parish, we come together to pray. We celebrate the sacraments. We care for those in need. We learn to live as followers of Jesus.

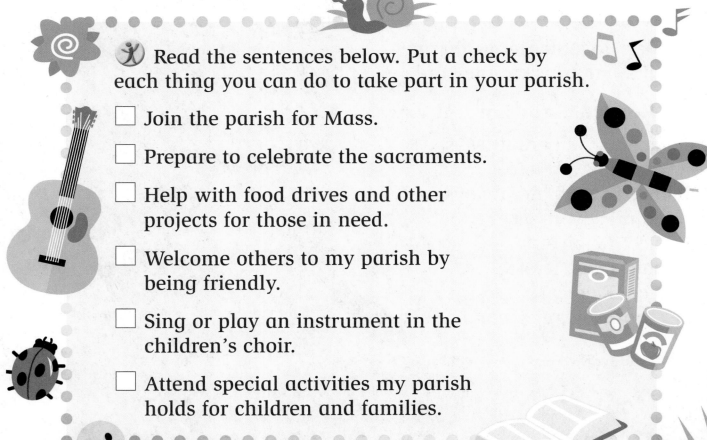

🕴 Read the sentences below. Put a check by each thing you can do to take part in your parish.

☐ Join the parish for Mass.

☐ Prepare to celebrate the sacraments.

☐ Help with food drives and other projects for those in need.

☐ Welcome others to my parish by being friendly.

☐ Sing or play an instrument in the children's choir.

☐ Attend special activities my parish holds for children and families.

A parish has a pastor who is chosen by the bishop. The **pastor** is the priest who leads and serves the parish. He leads the parish in celebrating the sacraments, in prayer, and in teaching.

Together with the pastor, the members of the parish continue the work of Jesus. Some of these people help in parish ministries. Together the whole parish serves the needs of others, especially those who are poor, sick, or lonely.

WE RESPOND

Complete the following.

I belong to _____ parish.

My pastor is _____.

In our parish we continue the work of Jesus

by _____

_____.

261

Bishops lead and serve the Church.

WE GATHER

✝ *Jesus, bless our parish community.*

Would you like to be the leader of a group you belong to? Why or why not?

What does a good leader do?

WE BELIEVE

Jesus chose the twelve Apostles to lead and care for his followers. He chose the Apostle Peter to be the leader of the Apostles. Peter and the other Apostles were the first leaders of the Church. They led the Church in continuing the work of Jesus.

Peter and the Apostles chose other men to lead and serve the Church. These leaders became known as bishops. Bishops still lead and serve the Church today. **Bishops** are leaders of the Church who carry on the work of the Apostles.

A bishop is chosen by the pope to lead and care for a diocese. A **diocese** is an area of the Church led by a bishop. A diocese is made up of all the Catholics who live in a certain area.

The bishop guides and serves the members of his diocese. He passes on the teachings of Jesus. He helps the people to grow closer to God.

Use the code. What are we part of?

A	C	D	E	H	I	O	P	R	S	U
1	2	3	4	5	6	7	8	9	10	11

A Catholic is part of a ____ ____ ____ ____ ____ ____,
              8   1   9   6   10   5

which is part of a ____ ____ ____ ____ ____ ____ ____,
            3   6   7   2   4   10   4

which is part of the ____ ____ ____ ____ ____ ____.
            2   5   11   9   2   5

bishops leaders of the Church who carry on the work of the Apostles

diocese an area of the Church led by a bishop

WE RESPOND

What diocese is your parish part of? My parish is part of the diocese of

_____.

How can we show others that we are part of the Church?

263

The pope is the leader of the Church.

WE GATHER

✝ *Jesus, guide the leaders of the Church.*

Pope Francis

🏃 Act out some things Saint Peter did to lead the Church.

WE BELIEVE

The pope is the Bishop of Rome in Italy. The **pope** is the leader of the Church who continues the work of Saint Peter. With the other bishops, the pope helps Catholics to be disciples of Jesus.

The pope serves and cares for the Church. He preaches the Good News of Jesus Christ to everyone. Wherever he is, the pope celebrates Mass and talks to the people.

The pope travels to other countries. The pope listens to the people's problems. He sees the good things they are doing for others. He asks them to love and care for one another. He teaches them about God's love and forgiveness.

Key Word

pope the leader of the Church who continues the work of Saint Peter

The pope lives in a special part of Rome called Vatican City. Vatican Radio sends out its programs in forty different languages so everyone who listens can understand. Every day the pope's messages and other programs about Jesus and the Catholic faith can be heard on Vatican Radio. Vatican Radio programming is broadcasted on the radio and over the Internet on the Vatican's own Web site at www.vatican.va.

Listen to the pope's message on Vatican Radio or log on to the Vatican's Web site.

WE RESPOND

If the pope were coming to your parish, what would you want to ask him?

_____

_____

What would you want to tell him?

_____

_____

The Church is in every part of the world.

WE GATHER

✝ *Holy Spirit, let us live in peace with all your people.*

Tell about some things your family does each year to celebrate holidays and birthdays.

WE BELIEVE

Catholics live in every part of the world. Catholics everywhere have the same beliefs.

These Catholics are Polish. It is Christmas Eve. The father of this Catholic family is breaking a wafer made of wheat called *oplatki (ō plát key)*. He will give a piece of the wafer to each member of his family. Sharing oplatki is a sign of love and peace.

These Catholics are celebrating the Feast of Corpus Christi, or the Feast of the Body and Blood of Christ. The priest is carrying the Eucharist for all to worship. The priest and people sing songs to Jesus as they walk through the streets of their town in a procession.

Catholics share and celebrate the same beliefs about the Blessed Trinity. They share the same beliefs about Jesus, the Son of God, the Church, Mary and the saints. They all celebrate the Eucharist and the other sacraments. They look to the pope as the leader of the Church.

However, Catholics around the world also show their faith in different ways.

Look at the pictures on these pages. Then read the sentences about each picture. You will learn some of the different ways Catholics pray and show their faith.

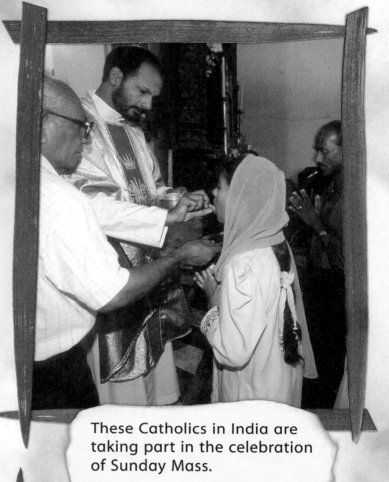

These Catholics in India are taking part in the celebration of Sunday Mass.

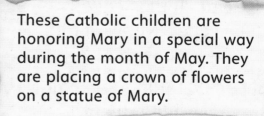

These Catholic children are honoring Mary in a special way during the month of May. They are placing a crown of flowers on a statue of Mary.

WE RESPOND

What could you tell a second grade class from another country about the way your parish prays and celebrates?

PROJECT

Show What *you* Know

| pastor |
| bishop |
| diocese |
| pope |

Use the Key Words to fill in the blanks. Write the missing letters in the spaces.

A p ___ ___ ___ ___ ___ leads the parish.

A b ___ ___ ___ ___ ___ leads the d ___ ___ ___ ___ ___.

The p ___ ___ ___ leads the whole Church.

Fast Facts

During the Mass, priests wear special clothes called vestments. They wear an alb, a stole, and a chasuble.

↳**DISCIPLE CHALLENGE** The color of the chasuble tells us something about the Church season. Notice the color of the priest's chasuble at Mass this week.

alb

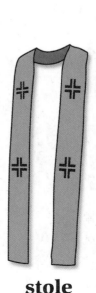

stole

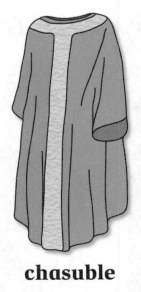

chasuble

DISCIPLE

Pray
Learn
Celebrate
Share
Choose
Live

Make it Happen

Missionaries teach others about Jesus. They follow Jesus' example. We can be missionaries in our homes, schools, neighborhoods, and world. We can share our belief in Jesus and live as he did. Make a banner that shares your belief in Jesus.

Picture This

Look at the picture of the children celebrating their faith. Then draw a picture of yourself celebrating your faith.

Take Home

Interview friends and relatives about the different ways their families might have celebrated their faith. Write questions to ask.

_____

_____

_____

CHAPTER TEST

Use the words in the box to complete the sentences.

1. A _____ is a community of Catholics who worship and work together.

2. The _____ is the leader of the Church who continues the work of Saint Peter.

3. A _____ is a leader of the Church who carries on the work of the Apostles.

4. A _____ is an area of the Church led by a bishop.

pope

bishop

diocese

parish

Circle the correct answer.

5. Is a pastor the Bishop of Rome?   **Yes**   **No**

6. Do Catholics around the world have different beliefs about the Blessed Trinity?   **Yes**   **No**

7. Did Jesus choose Peter to be the leader of the Apostles?   **Yes**   **No**

8. Do Catholics around the world show their faith in different ways?   **Yes**   **No**

9–10. Write two things all Catholics share and celebrate.

_____

_____

✞ We Gather in Prayer

Leader: The Lord be with you.

All: And with your spirit.

Leader: Lift up your hearts.

All: We lift them up to the Lord.

Leader: Let us give thanks to the Lord our God.

All: It is right and just.

🎵 Sing Hosanna

Sing hosanna! Sing hosanna!
Sing it for Jesus. Sing it for Jesus.
Sing it for friendship.
Sing it for friendship.

Sing it forever. Sing it forever.
Sing hosanna! Sing hosanna!
Sing hosanna! Sing!

Play the conga! Play the conga!
Play it for Jesus. Play it for Jesus.
Play it for friendship.
Play it for friendship.

Play it forever. Play it forever.
Play the conga! Play the conga!
Play the conga drum!

Prayer keeps us close to God.

✝ *God, help us to talk to you.*

Why do you talk to other people?
Why do you listen to other people?

WE BELIEVE

God wants us to get to know him better.
We can grow closer to God through prayer.
Prayer is talking and listening to God.
No matter how we pray, God is with us.

We talk to God about
different things. We talk
to him when we are
happy and when we are
sad. We share the things

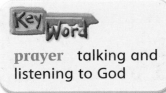

prayer talking and listening to God

we are thinking about. Sometimes we ask
for help or forgiveness. Other times we
thank him for his love, or ask his blessing.

God is always there to hear our prayer.
He listens to us. He knows what we need
and takes care of us.

Prayer is more than talking to God. We
listen to God, too. God speaks to us in
many ways. He speaks to us at Mass
and through the sacraments. He
speaks to us through the words
of the Bible. He speaks to us
through the leaders of
Church and through all of
those who show us his love.

WE RESPOND

Follow this prayer path. Answer the questions and pray along the way.

PRAYER PATH

PARISH

Who helps you to grow as a disciple of Jesus?

_____

Ask God to bless all those who share their faith with you.

NEIGHBORHOOD

Who in your neighborhood is in need?

_____

Pray for those in need that they may have strength and the things they need.

GOD'S CREATION

What are some gifts of creation that you use and enjoy?

_____

Praise God for his gifts of creation.

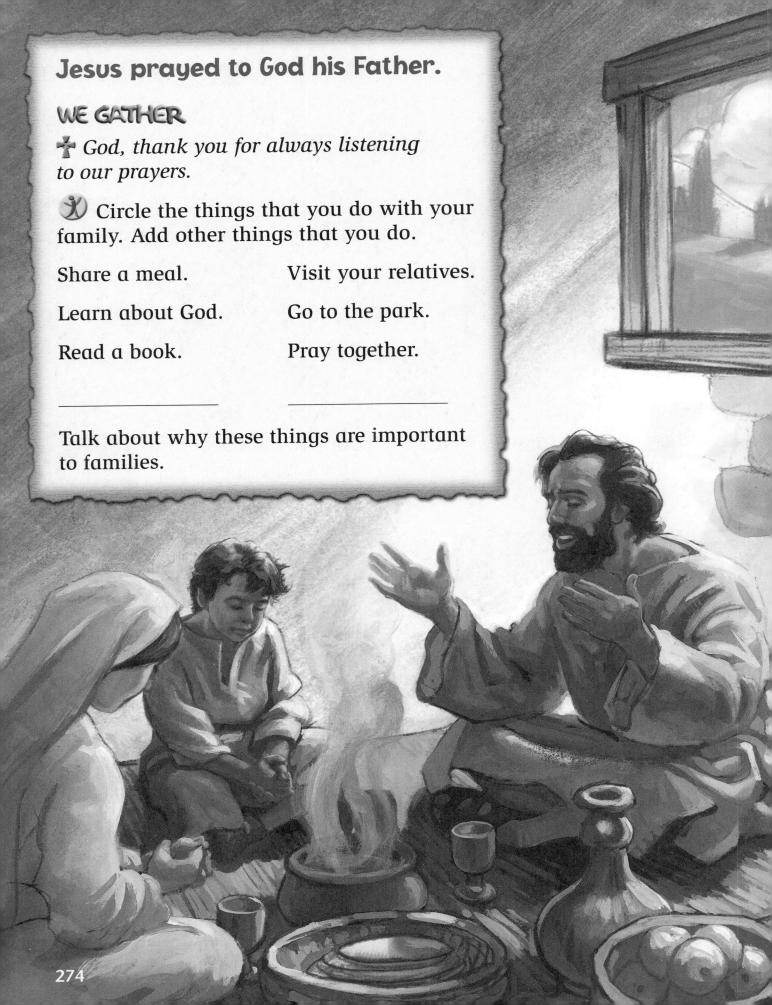

Jesus prayed to God his Father.

WE GATHER

✞ *God, thank you for always listening to our prayers.*

Circle the things that you do with your family. Add other things that you do.

Share a meal.	Visit your relatives.
Learn about God.	Go to the park.
Read a book.	Pray together.

_____   _____

Talk about why these things are important to families.

WE BELIEVE

Jesus, Mary, and Joseph were part of a family. When Jesus was growing up in Nazareth, he learned to pray. He prayed with Mary and Joseph. They prayed the prayers Jewish People had always prayed. They also gathered with other Jewish families to pray.

They all traveled to Jerusalem to celebrate religious holidays. The **Temple** is the holy place in Jerusalem where the Jewish People worshiped God.

As Jesus grew older he continued to pray. He wanted to be close to God his Father. He asked his Father to be with him. He thanked his Father for his many blessings.

Jesus often went off by himself to pray. Jesus also prayed when he was with his family, friends, and disciples.

Temple the holy place in Jerusalem where the Jewish People worshiped God

WE RESPOND

What are some times when you pray by yourself? How do you pray?

What are some times when you pray with others? How do you pray?

275

The Solitude of Christ, Maurice Denis/
© 2014 Artists Rights Society (ARS), New York

Jesus teaches us to pray.

WE GATHER

✝ *Jesus, help us to pray.*

Who are the people who have taught you to pray? What prayers did they teach you?

WE BELIEVE

Jesus' disciples knew that he loved and called on his Father. They saw how important prayer was to Jesus.

They wanted to learn how to pray as Jesus did. One day they asked Jesus, "Lord, teach us to pray." (Luke 11:1)

Jesus taught them this prayer.

The Lord's Prayer

Our Father, who art in heaven,

We talk to God. We praise him as our loving Father.

hallowed be thy name;

We say that God is holy. We honor and respect his name.

thy kingdom come; thy will be done on earth as it is in heaven.

We ask that all people will know and share God's love. This is what God wants for all of us.

Give us this day our daily bread;

We ask God to give us what we need. We remember all people who are hungry or poor.

and forgive us our trespasses as we forgive those who trespass against us;

We ask God to forgive us. We need to forgive others.

and lead us not into temptation, but deliver us from evil. Amen.

We ask God to keep us safe from anything that goes against his love.

This prayer is called the Lord's Prayer. It is also called the Our Father.

WE RESPOND

Our actions can also be prayers. How can you use actions to pray?

As a class make up prayerful actions for each of the parts of the Our Father. Then pray the prayer using the actions.

277

We pray as Jesus did.

WE GATHER

✝ *Jesus, be with us when we pray.*

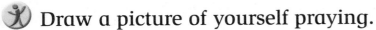 Draw a picture of yourself praying.

WE BELIEVE

We pray by ourselves and with others as Jesus did. There are many reasons to pray. We pray:

- to ask God for help
- to tell God how beautiful the world is
- to ask God to forgive us for hurting others
- to pray for someone who needs help or is sick
- to thank God for his love
- to ask for God's blessing for us and others.

When we pray we can use our own words. We can also use prayers that we have learned at home, in school, or in our parish. We use many of these prayers when we pray together.

Praying together is an important part of being a member of the Church. As a parish we join together to celebrate the Eucharist and the other sacraments.

There are other times when our parish prays together. Talk about some of these times.

WE RESPOND

Think about one way you and your family will pray with your parish this week.

Now sit quietly. Talk and listen to God.

PROJECT

Show What you Know

Write the Key Words into the word shapes.

prayer

Temple

Talking and listening to God

The holy place in Jerusalem where the Jewish People worshiped God

More to Explore

People in religious communities live a life of prayer. They pray together at different hours each day. They also spend time alone to think about and pray to God. Their prayers are very important to the Church and the world.

DISCIPLE

Pray
Learn
Celebrate
Share
Choose
Live

Pray Today

Choose the correct way through the maze by praying the Our Father.

Our Father, who art in heaven, hallowed be thy name;

Give us this day our daily bread;

thy kingdom come; thy will be done on earth as it is in heaven.

and forgive us our trespasses as we forgive those who trespass against us;

and lead us not into temptation; but deliver us from evil.

Amen.

Take Home

Learn this prayer as a family. Pray it together in the evenings.

Evening Prayer
Dear God, before we go to sleep, we want to thank you for this day so full of your kindness and your joy. We close our eyes to rest safe in your loving care.

Make it Happen

What is your favorite prayer? Share it.

CHAPTER TEST

Circle the correct answer.

1. Did Jesus always pray by himself? **Yes** **No**

2. Is prayer talking and listening to God? **Yes** **No**

3. Is the Hail Mary the prayer Jesus taught to his disciples? **Yes** **No**

4. Can we use our own words to pray? **Yes** **No**

Fill in the circle beside the correct answer.

5. God _____ listens to our prayer.
   ○ always   ○ sometimes

6. Praying together is _____ part of being a member of the Church.
   ○ not an important   ○ an important

7. Another name for the Lord's Prayer is the _____.
   ○ Hail Mary   ○ Our Father

8. Prayer was _____ to Jesus.
   ○ not important   ○ important

9–10. Write two things we ask God when we pray the Lord's Prayer.

_____

_____

25

We Honor Mary and the Saints

✝ We Gather in Prayer

♪ Litany of Saints

Holy Mary, Mother of God,
Holy Mary, born without sin,
Holy Mary, taken into heaven:

Chorus
Pray for us.
Pray with us.
Help us to share God's love.

Saint Peter and Saint Paul,
Saint Mary Magdalene,
Saint Catherine of Siena: (Chorus)

The Church honors the saints.

WE GATHER

✝ *Jesus, thank you for the people who show us your love.*

What does it mean to honor someone?
What are some ways we honor people?

_____

_____

_____

Saint Catherine of Siena

Saint John Bosco

WE BELIEVE

God is good and holy and wants us to be holy, too. So he shares his life with us especially in the sacraments. The sacraments help us to be holy. Loving God and others helps us to be holy, too.

The Church community honors holy people. The saints are holy people. The **saints** are all the members of the Church who have died and are happy with God forever in Heaven.

The saints loved God very much. They followed Jesus' example. They were kind and caring. They shared God's love with others.

We remember what the saints did and try to follow their example. Here are some of the saints we remember.

- Saint Peter and Saint Paul helped the Church to spread and grow.

- Saint Brigid of Ireland and Saint Catherine of Siena were peacemakers.

- Saint Rose of Lima and Saint Martin de Porres helped the poor and the sick.

- Saint John Bosco and Saint Frances Cabrini began schools to teach children about God's love.

How can you follow their example?

saints all the members of the Church who have died and are happy with God forever in Heaven

Saint Frances Cabrini

WE RESPOND

Who are some of the other saints you have learned about?

Write one of the saints' names on the line.

_____

Write a sentence to tell how you will follow this person's example.

_____

_____

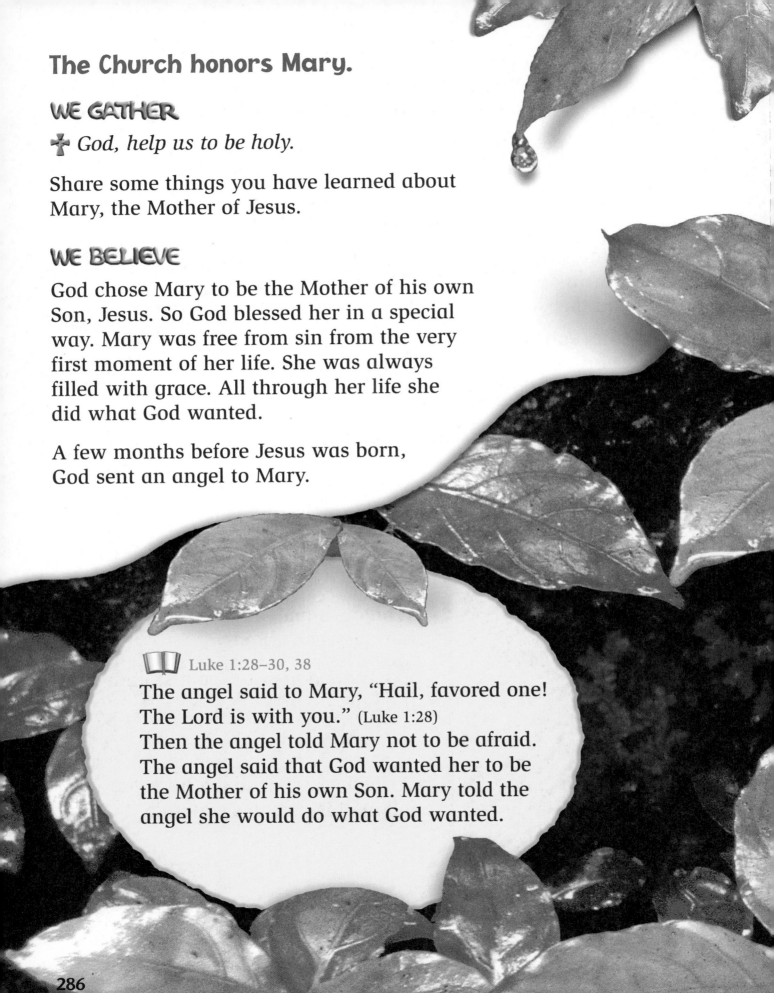

The Church honors Mary.

WE GATHER

✝ *God, help us to be holy.*

Share some things you have learned about Mary, the Mother of Jesus.

WE BELIEVE

God chose Mary to be the Mother of his own Son, Jesus. So God blessed her in a special way. Mary was free from sin from the very first moment of her life. She was always filled with grace. All through her life she did what God wanted.

A few months before Jesus was born, God sent an angel to Mary.

Luke 1:28–30, 38

The angel said to Mary, "Hail, favored one! The Lord is with you." (Luke 1:28)
Then the angel told Mary not to be afraid. The angel said that God wanted her to be the Mother of his own Son. Mary told the angel she would do what God wanted.

Mary is Jesus' mother. Jesus loved and honored her. We love and honor Mary as our mother, too. Mary is a holy woman. She is the greatest of saints. She is an example for all of Jesus' disciples.

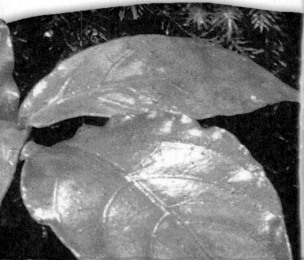

Use this code to find what we sometimes call Mary.

B	D	E	H	L	M	O	R	S	T
1	2	3	4	5	6	7	8	9	10

We call Mary the

__ __ __ __ __ __ __
1   5   3   9   9   3   2

__ __ __ __ __ __.
6   7   10   4   3   8

WE RESPOND

How can we honor Mary as the greatest saint?

Pray quietly. Thank Mary for being the Mother of the Son of God.

287

We honor Mary with special prayers.

WE GATHER

✝ *Holy Mary, we love you.*

What do families do to get ready for babies before they are born?

WE BELIEVE

Mary had a cousin named Elizabeth. Elizabeth was older than Mary. Elizabeth was going to have a baby, too. Mary went to visit her cousin and help her.

📖 Luke 1:39, 40–42

When Elizabeth saw Mary, she was very happy and excited. The Holy Spirit helped Elizabeth to know that God had chosen Mary to be the Mother of his own Son.

Elizabeth said to Mary, "Most blessed are you among women, and blessed is the fruit of your womb." (Luke 1:42) These words to Mary are part of one of the Church's prayers. We call this prayer the Hail Mary.

Add your own decorations to the prayer frame. Underline Elizabeth's words to Mary.

Hail Mary

Hail Mary, full of grace,
the Lord is with you!
Blessed are you among women,
and blessed is the fruit of your womb,
 Jesus.
Holy Mary, Mother of God,
pray for us sinners,
now and at the hour of our death.
Amen.

As Catholics...

The Rosary is a prayer in honor of Mary. When we pray the Rosary, we use beads as we pray. We begin with the Sign of the Cross, the Apostles' Creed, Our Father, three Hail Marys, and a Glory Be to the Father. Then there are five sets of ten beads to pray Hail Marys. Each set begins with the Our Father and ends with the Glory Be to the Father.

As we pray each set of ten beads, we think about the lives of Jesus and Mary.

Plan a time this week to pray the Rosary with your family.

WE RESPOND

What do you think Elizabeth's words to Mary might be today?

Pray the Hail Mary now.

We honor Mary on special days.

WE GATHER

✝ *Blessed Mother of God, pray for us.*

What are some different ways families thank mothers and grandmothers for all that they do?

WE BELIEVE

Catholics honor Mary in different ways during the year. On special days, called feast days, the whole parish gathers for Mass. Here are some of Mary's feast days.

Date	We gather to celebrate
January 1	Mary is the Mother of God.
August 15	Mary is in Heaven with God forever.
December 8	Mary was free from sin from the very first moment of her life.

Sometimes parish communities gather to honor Mary in special ways. They may have a procession. A **procession** is a prayer walk. While walking, people pray and sing. On December 12, many parishes have a procession to honor Mary as Our Lady of Guadalupe.

Key Word

procession a prayer walk

Inside and outside homes and churches, people often put statues and pictures of Mary. Looking at the statues and pictures can help people to remember Mary.

WE RESPOND

🎵 Immaculate Mary

Immaculate Mary,
your praises we sing.
You reign now in heaven
with Jesus our King.
Ave, Ave, Ave, Maria!
Ave, Ave, Maria!

What can your class do to honor Mary? Write your ideas.

_____

_____

_____

Pray Learn Celebrate Share Choose Live

PROJECT

Show What *you* Know

Find the **Key Words** hidden in the word search.

```
P R A Y I S X I O N
A O T X J A S H O S
N C D P M I R U J T
T E H S Y N L P A Z
B Y C A N T Q T S A
P R O C E S S I O N
```

saints

procession

Saint Stories

Saint Frances of Rome, Italy, took food to those who were poor. She comforted people who were sad and lonely. She cared for children who had no families. Her feast day is March 9.

DISCIPLE

Pray
Learn
Celebrate
Share
Choose
Live

Make it Happen

Mary is the greatest of saints. Make a card to honor Mary. Share it with your parish.

Pray Today

Pray the Hail Mary quietly with a friend.

↳ **DISCIPLE CHALLENGE** Talk together about what "full of grace" means.

Take Home

As a family, find paintings and stained-glass windows and other works of art that tell us about Mary. Visit your parish church or look online. Choose your family favorite. Write about it here.

_____

_____

_____

CHAPTER TEST

Fill in the circle beside the correct answer.

1. Mary _____ did what God wanted.

○ always   ○ never

2. Mary was free from _____ from the first moment of her life.

○ work   ○ sin

3. _____ told Mary that God wanted her to be the Mother of his own Son.

○ Elizabeth   ○ An angel

4. Mary is the _____ saint.

○ greatest   ○ newest

Complete the following sentences.

5. _____ is one of the Church's prayers to Mary.

6. A procession is a _____.

7. _____ are all the members of the Church who have died and are happy with God forever in Heaven.

8. Feast days are ways to _____ Mary.

9–10. **Write two ways you can follow the example of Mary and the saints.**

_____

We Show Love and Respect

26

✝ We Gather in Prayer

Leader: Let us listen to these words from one of Saint Paul's letters.

Reader: "Love is patient, love is kind. Love never fails. Faith, hope, love remain, these three; but the greatest of these is love."

(1 Corinthians 13:4, 8, 13)

The Word of the Lord.

All: Thanks be to God.

Leader: Now let us form a circle and sing.

🎵 A Circle of Love

Chorus
A circle of love, yes a circle of love;
each hand in a hand, a circle of
friends.
A circle of love that is open to all;
we open the circle and welcome
each one of you in.

Each person has something to bring:
a song, a story, a smile, a teardrop,
a dream, and loving to share. (Chorus)

We live in God's love.

WE GATHER

✝ *God, fill us with your love.*

When do people give gifts?
Why do they give gifts?

WE BELIEVE

The world we live in is God's gift to us. God has given us many gifts. He has given us creation. He has given us laws to know and love him. He has given us his Word in the Bible. He has given us the Church to help and guide us.

However, God's greatest gift is the gift of his Son, Jesus. Jesus gives us a share in God's life and love. We call this grace. We receive grace each time we celebrate the sacraments. We are strengthened by the Holy Spirit. We are filled with the gifts of faith, hope, and charity. These virtues are sources of prayer.

The gift of faith helps us to believe in God—the Father, the Son, and the Holy Spirit. We believe in God and all that he has done for us.

The gift of hope makes it easier to trust. We trust in Jesus and in God's promise to love us always.

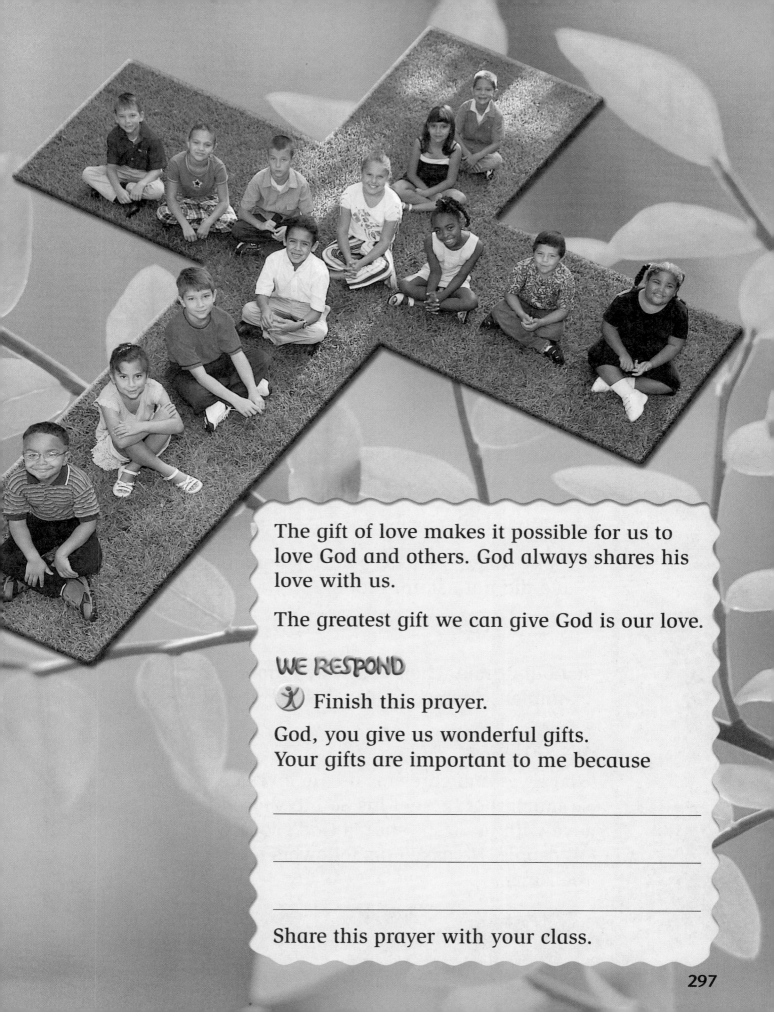

The gift of love makes it possible for us to love God and others. God always shares his love with us.

The greatest gift we can give God is our love.

WE RESPOND

Finish this prayer.

God, you give us wonderful gifts.
Your gifts are important to me because

_____

_____

_____

Share this prayer with your class.

Jesus taught us to love others.

WE GATHER

✝ *Jesus, we praise you for your love.*

Do you think these things would set a good example for others? Circle YES or NO.

• Joshua and his four-year-old brother share a room. When Joshua comes home, he always throws his clothes and books all over the room.

       YES   NO

• Vanessa sees her older sister pray before Mass starts.

       YES   NO

• Ricky raked the leaves for his neighbor and did not ask for money.

       YES   NO

Act out a time when you were a good example for someone else.

WE BELIEVE

God loves and cares for us. He loves us so much that he sent his Son to share his love with us. Jesus shared God's love with all people. He asked his followers to do the same.

Jesus taught his followers to love God and one another. He showed us the way to:

- pray to the Father
- live as a family
- be a friend and neighbor
- love and respect those who were poor, sick, and lonely.

 Look at these pictures of Jesus. How is Jesus showing love? How can you follow Jesus' example?

Jesus spent a lot of time talking with his followers. He loved them very much. He asked them to follow his example of love.

📖 John 13:34–35

Jesus said, "I give you a new commandment: love one another. As I have loved you, so you also should love one another. This is how all will know that you are my disciples, if you have love for one another." (John 13:34–35)

Jesus' **new commandment** is to love one another as he has loved us.

WE RESPOND

What will you do this week to show you are a disciple of Jesus?

new commandment Jesus' commandment to love one another as he has loved us

299

We love and respect others.

WE GATHER

✝ *Holy Spirit, help us to live as Jesus did.*

Who are some of the people you love?
What are some signs of your love for them?

WE BELIEVE

Loving as Jesus did brings us closer to
God and one another.

We show our belief in God by loving and
respecting him. We honor God's name as
a sign of our love. Together we worship
God. We remember all his gifts. We thank
God for all he has done for us.

Following Jesus' new commandment helps
us to follow all of God's commandments.

Circle every third letter to finish Jesus' new commandment. Write the words on the lines.

B I L T C O P L V S X E Q Z D   A G Y N F O S I U

A B L E I O P S V Z Y E   U T O W A N L I E

Y E A R S N Q U O H E T R C H I O E L M R

"As I have __ __ __ __ __   __ __ __,

so you also should __ __ __ __   __ __ __

__ __ __ __ __ __ __." (John 13:34)

When we follow Jesus' words, we try to love our family, friends, and all people as he did. We respect and obey our parents and all those who take care of us. We thank our families and friends for their love and help. We also try to be kind, fair, and truthful. We share the things we have. We respect the belongings of other people.

WE RESPOND

Sit quietly and think about ways you can follow Jesus' new commandment.

I will follow Jesus' new commandment today by

_____

We respect God's creation.

WE GATHER

✝ *God, what wonders are in your creation!*

What are some things that you take care of?
What are some things your family takes care of? What things do people in your neighborhood take care of?

WE BELIEVE

God asks us to respect his gift of creation. God created the land and the sea, the sun, moon, and stars. God created all the animals and plants. He created us, too! All that God created is good.

🎵 God Made the World

God made the world so broad and grand,
   filled it with blessings from his hand.
God made the sky so high and blue,
   and all the little children too.

God made the sun, the moon and stars,
   lighting the world from near and far.
God made the world with tender care
   and all the little children there.

God made the sparrow and the rose,
   gifts for the ear, the eye and nose.
God made the beauty voices bring,
   when all the little
   children sing.

People have a special place in God's creation. God has asked us to take care of his gifts of creation.

We care for the world. We protect all that God created. We work together to share the goodness of creation.

We can find the things God created in our backyards, our neighborhoods, our cities, and in every country. The gifts of God's creation are everywhere!

As Catholics...

The gifts of creation belong to all people everywhere. Everyone should have food to eat and clean water to drink. However, there are many parts of the world where people are hungry and thirsty. So we share what we have. We also help them to grow food and find water. This is part of what it means to care for God's creation.

Find out what your neighborhood is doing to take care of God's creation.

WE RESPOND

Put a check (✓) in front of the ways you will take care of God's creation this week.

☐ feed and care for my pet

☐ put trash in a can

☐ recycle cans, bottles, and papers

☐ turn off the water

☐ plant new trees

Now add two more ways you will help care for creation next week.

_____

_____

PROJECT

Pray
Learn
Celebrate
Share
Choose
Live

Show What *you* Know

Circle the picture of the children following
Jesus' new commandment.

Picture This

Draw a picture showing a way that you
respect God's creation.

DISCIPLE

Pray
Learn
Celebrate
Share
Choose
Live

Make it Happen

Tell your family what the gifts of faith, hope, and love help us to do. To help you prepare, complete this organizer.

| The gift of faith | helps us to | |

| The gift of hope | helps us to | |

| The gift of _____ | helps us to | love God and others. |

What's the Word?

Read these words from one of Saint Paul's letters.

"Love is patient,
love is kind.
It is not jealous . . .
it is not rude." (1 Corinthians 13:4–5)

Tell how this is true. **Now, pass it on!**

Take Home

As a family share ways you have learned to be disciples of Jesus this year!

CHAPTER TEST

Fill in the circle beside the correct answer.

1. Jesus shared God's love with _____ people.
   - ○ all
   - ○ a few
   - ○ some

2. Jesus' new commandment is to love one another as _____ loved us.
   - ○ his followers
   - ○ his neighbors
   - ○ he

3. _____ have a special place in God's creation.
   - ○ Plants
   - ○ People
   - ○ Animals

4. God's greatest gift to us is his _____.
   - ○ Son
   - ○ creation
   - ○ law

5. God's gift of _____ helps us to believe in God and all that he has done for us.
   - ○ faith
   - ○ hope
   - ○ love

6. God's gift of _____ helps us to trust in Jesus and in God's promise to love us always.
   - ○ faith
   - ○ hope
   - ○ love

7–8. Write two ways Jesus showed us how to love God and others.

_____

9–10. Write two ways we can follow Jesus' new commandment.

_____

Christ has risen, Alleluia!

SEASONAL
CHAPTER 27

This chapter celebrates the entire
Easter season.

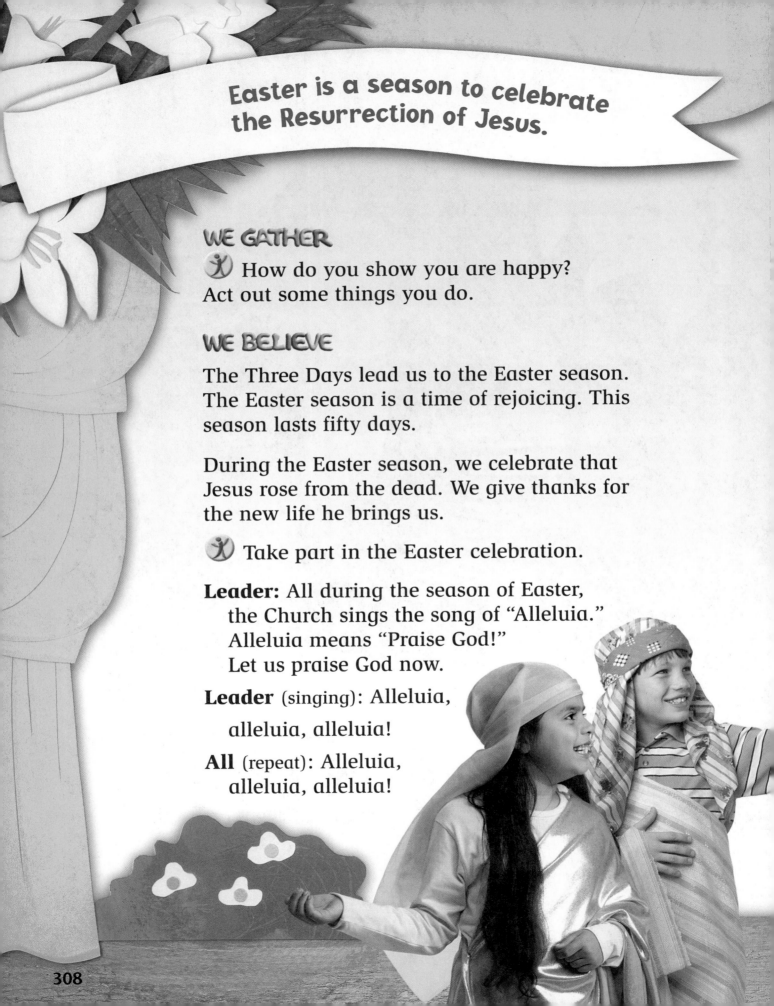

Easter is a season to celebrate the Resurrection of Jesus.

WE GATHER

How do you show you are happy? Act out some things you do.

WE BELIEVE

The Three Days lead us to the Easter season. The Easter season is a time of rejoicing. This season lasts fifty days.

During the Easter season, we celebrate that Jesus rose from the dead. We give thanks for the new life he brings us.

Take part in the Easter celebration.

Leader: All during the season of Easter, the Church sings the song of "Alleluia." Alleluia means "Praise God!" Let us praise God now.

Leader (singing): Alleluia, alleluia, alleluia!

All (repeat): Alleluia, alleluia, alleluia!

📖 Luke 24:1–9

Reader 1: On the first day of the week, at dawn, the women went to the tomb. They were bringing spices to bless Jesus' body. They found the stone rolled away. The body of Jesus was gone!

Reader 2: While they stood there, two angels appeared beside them. The women were frightened.

Angel 1: Are you looking for Jesus? He is not here. He has been raised up.

Angel 2: Remember what Jesus told you. He said that he would give his life for us. He would be crucified. He said that on the third day he would rise again.

Reader 3: Then the women were filled with joy. They ran back to tell the other disciples what they had seen and heard.

All (singing): Alleluia, alleluia, alleluia!

EASTER

Like the women at the tomb, we go and tell others about Jesus' Resurrection. We want them to know the Good News that Jesus died and rose for all people. We want to share the joy that comes from believing in Jesus.

WE RESPOND

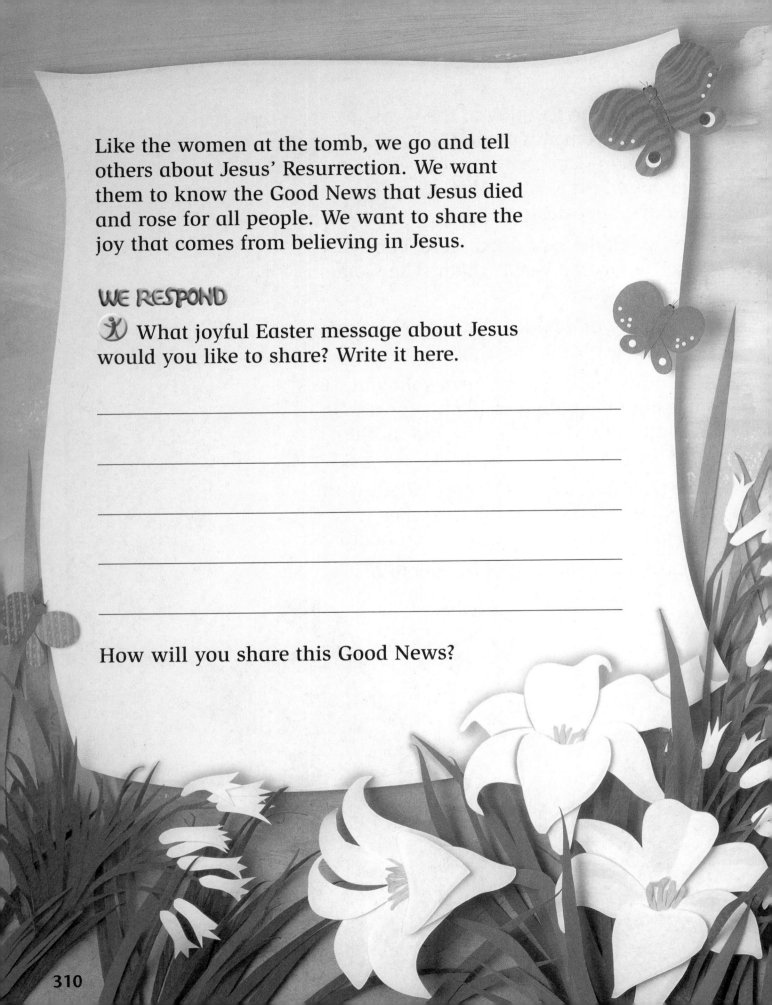 What joyful Easter message about Jesus would you like to share? Write it here.

_____

_____

_____

_____

_____

How will you share this Good News?

✝ We Respond in Prayer

Leader: Jesus, we know you are alive and with us today. Alleluia!

Reader 1: Give thanks to the Lord, for he is good, for his mercy lasts forever, alleluia!

All: This is the day the Lord has made; let us rejoice and be glad.

Reader 2: Set your heart on Jesus Christ, for he is risen, alleluia!

All: This is the day the Lord has made; let us rejoice and be glad.

Reader 3: This we believe, alleluia, alleluia, alleluia!

All: This is the day the Lord has made; let us rejoice and be glad.

🎵 This Is the Day

This is the day, this is the day
that the Lord has made,
that the Lord has made;
we will rejoice, we will rejoice and
be glad in it, and be glad in it.

This is the day
that the Lord has made;
we will rejoice
and be glad in it.
This is the day, this is the
day that the Lord has made.

EASTER

311

PROJECT DISCIPLE

Pray Learn Celebrate Share Choose Live

Show What *you* Know

Unscramble the words to find an important hidden message.

> **season of to celebrate is a Easter Resurrection the Jesus.**

_____

_____

Celebrate!

Announce the Good News. Jesus is risen! Decorate this bumper sticker to share the joy of Easter with others.

Take Home

During the Easter season, the Church often prays three alleluias in a row, instead of just one. Add Easter joy to meal prayers or evening prayers.
Try praying three alleluias after the Amen. Practice now. Say, "alleluia, alleluia, alleluia!"

Fill in the circle beside the correct answer.

1. A _____ is an area of the Church led by a bishop.
   ○ diocese   ○ parish   ○ neighborhood

2. _____ is talking and listening to God.
   ○ Penance   ○ Prayer   ○ Temple

3. The greatest saint is _____.
   ○ Mary   ○ Elizabeth   ○ Joseph

4. The _____ is the leader of the whole Church.
   ○ pope   ○ bishop   ○ pastor

Circle the correct answer.

5. Did Jesus teach his Apostles the Hail Mary?   **Yes**   **No**

6. Did Jesus choose Peter to lead the Apostles?   **Yes**   **No**

7. Do Catholics throughout the world believe in the Blessed Trinity?   **Yes**   **No**

8. Is God's greatest gift to us the gift of creation?   **Yes**   **No**

continued on next page

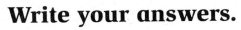

Write your answers.

9. Why do we pray?

_____

_____

_____

_____

_____

10. Why do we honor Mary?

_____

_____

_____

_____

The Lord's Prayer

Part 1 I Open My Heart

Jesus taught us to pray by the example he gave. He often went off alone to pray by himself, and he also prayed with his disciples. Jesus prayed in the Temple, in the mountains, in the garden, and on the Sea of Galilee. Jesus always made time for prayer, listening to his Father and the Holy Spirit.

Write a prayer to God that you can pray today, by yourself or with a friend. Make up movements to go with your prayer. Share your prayer with a partner.

Shepherds' Field, Bethlehem

The Lord's Prayer

Part 2 We Come Together for Prayer

Leader: Jesus, you taught us to call God "our Father." You promise us that God always hears our prayers and knows what we need.

Reader 1: Jesus "was praying . . . , and when he had finished, one of his disciples said to him, 'Lord, teach us to pray'" (Luke 11:1).

Reader 2: Jesus, you taught us to pray to God as our loving Father. Let us pray in the words that Jesus taught us:

All: Our Father, who art in heaven,
hallowed be thy name;
thy kingdom come;
thy will be done on earth
    as it is in heaven.
Give us this day our daily bread;
and forgive us our trespasses
as we forgive those
    who trespass against us;
and lead us not into temptation,
but deliver us from evil. Amen.

Sermon on the Mount, by W. J. Makowski

Leader: Father, hear our prayers. We trust in your love for us. We know that you always help us with our needs.

All: Thank you, Lord, for teaching us to pray. Amen.

The Lord's Prayer

Part 3 I Cherish God's Word

Before he chose his Apostles, Jesus "departed to the mountain to pray, and he spent the night in prayer to God" (Luke 6:12).

READ the quotation from Scripture. Read slowly. Pay close attention to what you are reading.

REFLECT on what you read. Think about:

- Why do you think Jesus prayed all night?

- When have you prayed about something over and over?

- What are some times when you need to pray?

SHARE your thoughts and feelings with God in prayer. Speak to God as a friend.

CONTEMPLATE, or sit quietly and think about God's Word in the Scripture passage from the Gospel of Luke above.

The Lord's Prayer

Part 4 I Value My Catholic Faith

When we pray, we ask God to care for our needs and the needs of all people. Work with a partner and look at each photo below. Talk about what the person in each photo might need. What do you think the person would pray for? Write this on the lines under each photo.

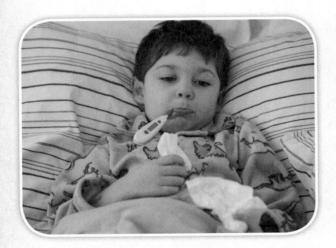

The Lord's Prayer

Part 5 I Celebrate Catholic Identity

In the Lord's Prayer, we pray, "Thy kingdom come; thy will be done on earth as it is in heaven." In these words we pray that people will live as God wants. They will love God and each other.

We can share God's love at home with our families. Draw one way you can share God's love at home.

The Lord's Prayer

Part 6 I Honor My Catholic Identity

Leader: Jesus teaches us to pray to God as our Father. Jesus asks us to remember that we are God's children. We can trust God our Father with all our needs. Let us pray the Litany of God the Father. A litany is a prayer made up of short titles for God, Jesus, or Mary or other saints. After each title, we pray a short response.

God the Father, Maker of heaven and earth,

All: Hear our prayer.

Leader: God the Son, Savior of all creation,

All: Have mercy on us.

Leader: God the Holy Spirit, Divine Love among us,

All: Have mercy on us.

Leader: Holy Trinity, one God,

All: Have mercy on us.

Leader: The Father, First Person of the Blessed Trinity,

All: Hear us and bless us.

Leader: Our Father in heaven,

All: Blessed is your name. Amen.

(By Philip Neri Powell, OP)

Catholic Identity Retreat

Bringing the Retreat Home

The Lord's Prayer

Retreat Recap

Review the pages of your child's *Celebrating Catholic Identity: Prayer* retreat. Ask your child to tell you about the retreat. Talk about the Lord's Prayer:

- Jesus showed us how to pray by his example.
- Jesus taught us to pray.
- Jesus taught us to call God our Father. He gave us the Lord's Prayer, also called the Our Father.

Our Father, Hear Our Prayer

In Part 6 of your child's retreat, your child prayed using the Litany of God the Father. Extend this litany as a family. Take turns adding titles for God that have "Father" in them. Also add titles for Jesus and the Holy Spirit. Write these down and then pray them together.

Our Litany

_____

_____

_____

_____

_____

_____

Take a Moment

Pray the Our Father together at mealtime or before bedtime. You may wish to review Chapter 24 of *We Believe* Grade 2 for further understanding of what each petition of the Our Father means.

Family Prayer

Pray together this prayer to God our Father.

Father,
keep before us the wisdom and love
you have revealed in your Son.
Help us to be like him
in word and deed,
for he lives and reigns with you and the
    Holy Spirit,
one God, forever and ever.
Amen.

(From *Morning Prayer, Liturgy of the Hours*)

For more resources, see the *Catholic Identity Home Companion* at the end of this book.

Why We Believe
As a Catholic Family

What if someone asks us:

- What beliefs and practices do all Catholics and Christians share?
- Why must we work toward Christian unity?

The following resources can help us to respond:

Catholics are Christians, and the Catholic Church works with other Christians to bring together all Christians. Some of the other Christian denominations include Orthodox Christians, Episcopal Christians, Lutherans, Methodists, Presbyterians, and Baptists. Our work toward unity with other Christians is called *ecumenism*.

Christians everywhere pray the Lord's Prayer, which is found in Matthew 6:9–13. The Lord's Prayer is one of several things Christians have in common. For example, all Christians are baptized. All Christians believe in and follow Jesus. Christians believe that God is Father, Son, and Holy Spirit. Christians also believe that Jesus is both divine and human, that Jesus died for our sins and rose again from the dead, and that the Holy Spirit inspired the Bible.

What does Scripture say?

Jesus said, "I pray not only for them, but also for those who will believe in me through their word, so that they may all be one, as you, Father, are in me and I in you, that they also may be in us, that the world may believe that you sent me" (John 17:20–21).

"I urge you, brothers, in the name of our Lord Jesus Christ, that all of you agree in what you say, and that there be no divisions among you, but that you be united in the same mind and in the same purpose."
(1 Corinthians 1:10)

As Catholics we believe that "the one Church of Christ . . . subsists in the Catholic Church, which is governed by the successor of Peter and by the Bishops in communion with him, although many elements of sanctification and of truth are found outside of its visible structure. These elements, as gifts belonging to the Church of Christ, are forces impelling toward catholic unity" (*Dogmatic Constitution on the Church*, 8).

Each year in January the Church celebrates the Week of Prayer for Christian unity. We pray that all Christians may be one.

What does the Church say?

"Christ always gives his Church the gift of unity, but the Church must always pray and work to maintain, reinforce, and perfect the unity that Christ wills for her." (CCC, 820)

The Church is "the one Body of Christ on earth to which all should be fully incorporated who belong in any way to the people of God" (Second Vatican Council, Unitatis Redintegratio (Decree on Ecumenism), 3).

"When we have become, not many members, but one spirit, then . . . 'God may be all and in all.'"
(Saint Ambrose, one of the Church Fathers, about A.D. 337–397)

Notes:

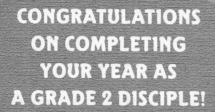

**CONGRATULATIONS
ON COMPLETING
YOUR YEAR AS
A GRADE 2 DISCIPLE!**

Fold on this line.

Pray
Learn
Celebrate
Share
Choose
Live

**A RECORD OF MY JOURNEY
AS A GRADE 2 DISCIPLE**

_____
Name

✂ Cut on this line.

Disciples of Jesus make loving choices.

This year, I made a loving choice

- in my family when I

_____.

- in my school when I

_____.

I can show love for others this summer by

_____.

Disciples of Jesus pray every day.

A prayer I like to pray

- by myself is

_____.

- with others is

_____.

My prayer for summer is

_____.

4

5

Disciples of Jesus learn about their faith.

One thing I learned this year

- about following Jesus is

_____.

- about sharing my faith with others is

_____.

✂ Cut on this line.

Disciples of Jesus share their faith with family.

My picture of a family member who helps me share my faith

Disciples of Jesus live out their faith.

This summer I will

❏ obey my parents

❏ take care of my pet

❏ play fairly with my friends

❏ help with family chores

❏ pray each day

❏ be kind to a neighbor

❏ _____.

Disciples of Jesus gather to celebrate.

This year,

I celebrated the Sacrament of

_____.

I celebrated the sacrament with

_____.

I celebrated the sacrament by

_____.

PROJECT DISCIPLE

End-of-Year Prayer Service

✝ We Gather in Prayer

Leader: We have learned many things about Jesus this year.

Group 1: Jesus is always with us.

Group 2: Jesus invites us to forgive.

Group 1: Jesus shares God's life with us.

Group 2: Jesus asks us to care for each other.

Leader: We ask Jesus to help us remember all of these good things.

All: Jesus, thank you for loving us.
Be with us this summer.
We want to share your Good News with everyone!

🎵 Take the Word of God with You

Take the peace of God with you
as you go.
Take the seeds of God's peace
and make them grow.

Go in peace to serve the world,
in peace to serve the world.
Take the love of God, the love of God
with you as you go.

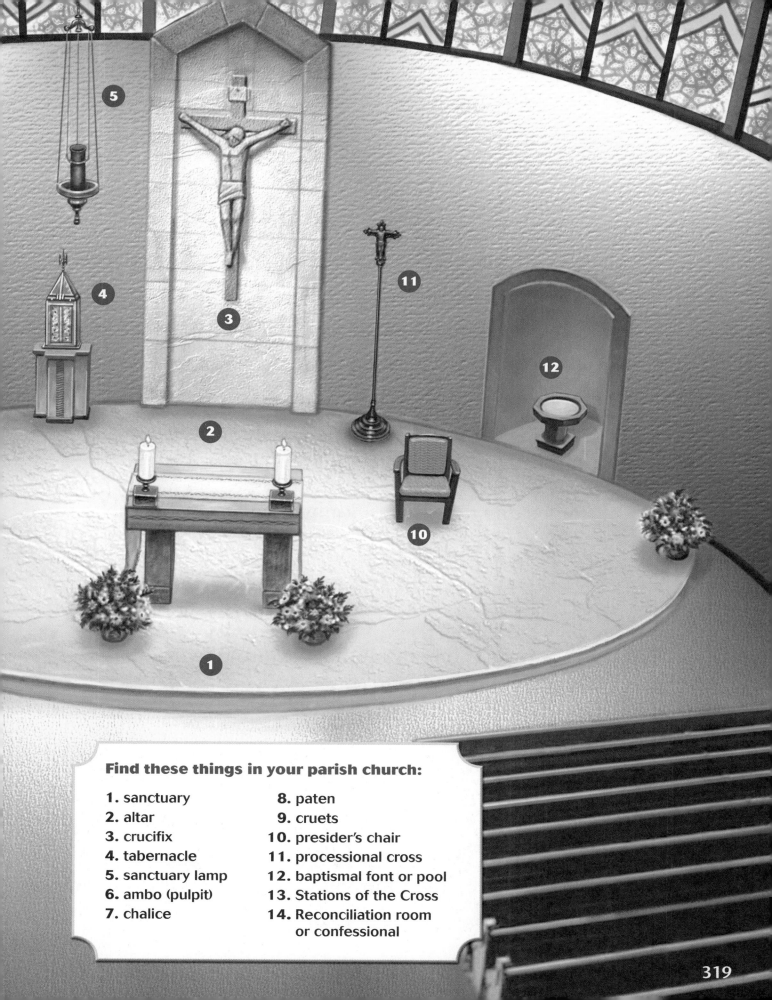

Find these things in your parish church:

1. sanctuary
2. altar
3. crucifix
4. tabernacle
5. sanctuary lamp
6. ambo (pulpit)
7. chalice
8. paten
9. cruets
10. presider's chair
11. processional cross
12. baptismal font or pool
13. Stations of the Cross
14. Reconciliation room or confessional

You are learning and living out ways to be a disciple of Jesus Christ.

Look what awaits you in:

WE BELIEVE **Grade 3: We Are the Church.**

You will learn about and live out that

- Jesus gives us the Church.
- We are members of the Church.
- The Church leads us in worship.
- We are called to discipleship.

Until next year, pay attention each time you go to Mass. Look around you. Listen.

Here is one thing that I know about the Church.

_____

_____

Here is one thing that I want to learn more about next year.

_____

_____

We are blessed to be members of the Church!

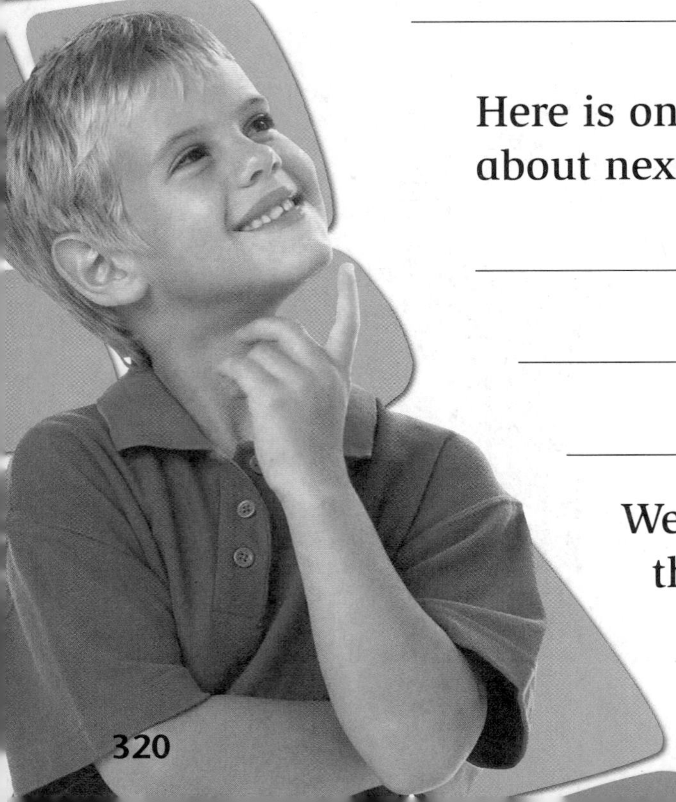

My Mass Book

Fold on this line.

Cut on this line.

The priest blesses us.
The priest or deacon may say,
"Go in peace."
We say,
"Thanks be to God."
We go out to live as
Jesus' followers.

We welcome one another.
We stand and sing.
We pray the Sign of the Cross.
The priest says,
"The Lord be with you."
We answer,
"And with your spirit."

We gather with our parish.
We remember and celebrate
what Jesus said and did at the
Last Supper.

Fold on this line.

Cut on this line.

We ask God and one another
for forgiveness.
We praise God as we sing,

**"Glory to God in the highest,
and on earth peace to
people of good will."**

Then the priest invites us to
share in the Eucharist.
As people receive the Body
and Blood of Christ, they
answer,

"Amen."

While this is happening, we
sing a song of thanks.

We get ready to receive Jesus. Together we pray or sing the Our Father. Then we share a sign of peace.
We say,
"Peace be with you."

Then the priest takes the cup of wine.
He says,
"TAKE THIS, ALL OF YOU, AND DRINK FROM IT, FOR THIS IS THE CHALICE OF MY BLOOD. . . ."

The Liturgy of the Word

We listen to two readings from the Bible.
After each one, the reader says, "The word of the Lord."
We answer,
"Thanks be to God."

We stand to say aloud what we believe as Catholics.
Then we pray for the Church and all people.
After each prayer we say,
"Lord, hear our prayer."

We stand and sing **Alleluia.**
The priest or deacon reads the
Gospel.
Then he says,
"The Gospel of the Lord."
We answer,
**"Praise to you,
Lord Jesus Christ."**

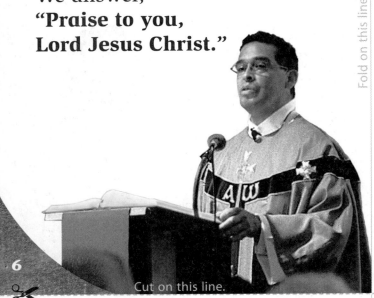

6

Fold on this line.

Cut on this line.

The Liturgy of the Eucharist

The priest prepares the altar.
People bring gifts of bread and
wine to the priest.
The priest prepares these gifts.
We pray,
"Blessed be God for ever."

8

We sing or pray,
"Amen."
We believe Jesus Christ is really
present in the Eucharist.

11

Then we remember what Jesus
said and did at the Last Supper.
The priest takes the bread.
He says,
"TAKE THIS, ALL OF YOU, AND
EAT OF IT, FOR THIS IS MY BODY,
WHICH WILL BE GIVEN UP FOR
YOU."

9

Angel of God

Angel of God,
my guardian dear,
to whom God's love
    commits me here,
ever this day be at my side,
to light and guard,
    to rule and guide.

Amen.

Find other versions of some of these prayers at **www.webelieveweb.com**

Fold on this line.

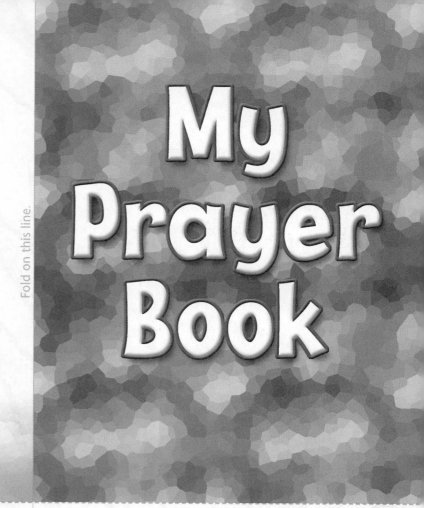

My Prayer Book

The Apostles' Creed

I believe in God the
    Father almighty,
    Creator of heaven and earth,

and in Jesus Christ, his only Son,
  our Lord,
  who was conceived by
  the Holy Spirit,
  born of the Virgin Mary,
suffered under Pontius Pilate,
  was crucified, died and
  was buried;
he descended into hell;
on the third day he rose again
  from the dead;

Glory Be to the Father

Glory be to the Father
and to the Son
and to the Holy Spirit,
as it was in the beginning
is now, and ever shall be
world without end. Amen.

Sign of the Cross

In the name of the Father,
and of the Son,
and of the Holy Spirit.

Amen.

Fold on this line.

he ascended into heaven,
    and is seated at the right hand
    of God the Father almighty;
from there he will come to judge
    the living and the dead.

I believe in the Holy Spirit,
    the holy catholic Church,
    the communion of saints,
    the forgiveness of sins,
    the resurrection of the body,
    and life everlasting.

Amen.

Cut on this line.

Our Father

Our Father, who art in heaven,
hallowed be thy name;
thy kingdom come;
thy will be done on earth as
    it is in heaven.
Give us this day our daily bread;
and forgive us our trespasses
as we forgive those who
    trespass against us;
and lead us not into temptation,
but deliver us from evil.

Amen.

Grace After Meals

We give you thanks
    almighty God
for these and all your gifts,
which we have received through
Christ our Lord.

Amen.

Grace Before Meals

Bless us, O Lord, and these
   your gifts
which we are about to receive
from your goodness.
Through Christ our Lord.

Amen.

Fold on this line.

Hail Mary

Hail Mary, full of grace,
the Lord is with you!
Blessed are you among women,
and blessed is the fruit of your
   womb, Jesus.
Holy Mary, Mother of God,
pray for us sinners,
now and at the hour of
   our death.

Amen.

Cut on this line.

Morning Offering

My God, I offer you today
all that I think and do and say,
uniting it with what was done
on earth, by Jesus Christ,
your Son.

I firmly intend, with your help,
to do penance,
to sin no more,
and to avoid whatever
   leads me to sin.
Our Savior Jesus Christ
suffered and died for us.
In his name, my God,
   have mercy.

Act of Contrition

My God,
I am sorry for my sins with
  all my heart.
In choosing to do wrong
and failing to do good,
I have sinned against you
whom I should love above
  all things.

Fold on this line.

Evening Prayer

Dear God, before I sleep
I want to thank you for this day
so full of your kindness
and your joy.
I close my eyes to rest
safe in your loving care.

Cut on this line.

Prayer Before the Blessed Sacrament

Jesus,
You are God-with-us,
especially in this Sacrament
of the Eucharist.
You love me as I am
and help me grow.

Come and be with me
in all my joys and sorrows.
Help me share your peace
and love
with everyone I meet.
I ask in your name.

Amen.

The Seven Sacraments

The Sacraments of Christian Initiation
> Baptism
> Confirmation
> Eucharist

The Sacraments of Healing
> Penance and Reconciliation
> Anointing of the Sick

The Sacraments at the Service of Communion
> Holy Orders
> Matrimony

The Ten Commandments

1. I am the LORD your God: you shall not have strange gods before me.
2. You shall not take the name of the LORD your God in vain.
3. Remember to keep holy the LORD's Day.
4. Honor your father and your mother.
5. You shall not kill.
6. You shall not commit adultery.
7. You shall not steal.
8. You shall not bear false witness against your neighbor.
9. You shall not covet your neighbor's wife.
10. You shall not covet your neighbor's goods.

Glossary

absolution (page 145)
God's forgiveness of our sins by the priest in the Sacrament of Penance

Apostles (page 33)
the twelve men chosen by Jesus to be the leaders of his disciples

assembly (page 189)
the community of people who join together for the celebration of the Mass

Baptism (page 59)
the sacrament in which we are freed from sin and given grace

Bible (page 97)
the book in which God's Word is written

bishops (page 263)
leaders of the Church who carry on the work of the Apostles

Blessed Sacrament (page 222)
another name for the Eucharist

Blessed Trinity (page 26)
the Three Persons in One God

called by God (page 249)
invited by God to love and serve him

Catholics (page 45)
baptized members of the Church, led and guided by the pope and bishops

Church (page 39)
all the people who are baptized in Jesus Christ and follow his teachings

commandments (page 109)
God's laws

confession (page 145)
telling our sins to the priest in the Sacrament of Penance

Confirmation (page 70)
the sacrament that seals us with the Gift of the Holy Spirit and strengthens us

conscience (page 136)
God's gift that helps us to know right from wrong

contrition (page 145)
being sorry for our sins and promising not to sin again

diocese (page 263)
an area of the Church led by a bishop

disciples (page 33)
those who follow Jesus

divine (page 25)
a word used to describe God

Eucharist (page 176)
the sacrament of the Body and Blood of Jesus Christ

Eucharistic Prayer (page 210)
the most important prayer of the Mass

faith (page 47)
a gift from God that helps us to trust God and believe in him

free will (page 122)
God's gift to us that allows us to make choices

Gospels (page 101)
four of the books in the New Testament that are about Jesus' teachings and his life on earth

grace (page 59)
God's life in us

Great Commandment (page 109)
Jesus' teaching to love God and others

Holy Communion (page 179)
receiving the Body and Blood of Christ

Holy Family (page 20)
the family of Jesus, Mary, and Joseph

homily (page 201)
the talk given by the priest or deacon at Mass that helps us understand the readings and how we are to live

Last Supper (page 175)
the meal Jesus shared with his disciples on the night before he died

Liturgy of the Eucharist (page 209)
the second main part of the Mass in which the gifts of bread and wine become the Body and Blood of Christ

Liturgy of the Word (page 197)
the first main part of the Mass when we listen to God's Word

Mass (page 179)
the celebration of the Eucharist

mercy (page 126)
God's love and forgiveness

mortal sins (page 124)
sins that break our friendship with God

new commandment (page 299)
Jesus' commandment to love one another as he has loved us

New Testament (page 101)
the second part of the Bible

Old Testament (page 99)
the first part of the Bible

Original Sin (page 59)
the first man and woman disobeyed God; the first sin

parishes (page 45)
communities that worship and work together

pastor (page 261)
the priest who leads and serves the parish

a penance (page 145)
a prayer or kind act we do to make up for our sins

Penance and Reconciliation (page 135)
the sacrament in which we receive and celebrate God's forgiveness of our sins

pope (page 264)
the leader of the Church who continues the work of Saint Peter

prayer (page 272)
talking and listening to God

procession (page 290)
a prayer walk

psalm (page 198)
a song of praise from the Bible

Resurrection (page 35)
Jesus' rising from the dead

sacrament (page 48)
a special sign given to us by Jesus

saints (page 285)
all the members of the Church who have died and are happy with God forever in Heaven

sin (page 124)
a thought, word, or act that we freely choose to commit even though we know that it is wrong

tabernacle (page 222)
the special place in the church in which the Blessed Sacrament is kept

Temple (page 275)
the holy place in Jerusalem where the Jewish People worshiped God

Ten Commandments (page 110)
ten special laws God gave to his people

venial sins (page 124)
sins that hurt our friendship with God

worship (page 47)
to give God thanks and praise

Index

The following is a list of topics that appear in the pupil's text.
Boldface indicates an entire chapter.

I n this section, you will find questions and answers that review the content in your *We Believe: Catholic Identity Edition* book this year. Each question in this section covers the key Catholic teachings in your book, in chapter order. Answer each question to review what you have learned—whether you use this section at home, in school, or in the parish. The answers provided will strengthen your understanding of your Catholic faith and help to reinforce your Catholic Identity.

The *CCC* references after each answer indicate where to find further information about that answer in the *Catechism of the Catholic Church.*

Q: Why did God send his Son, Jesus?

A: God sent his Son, Jesus, to be with us and to share God's great love with everyone. *CCC,* 457, 458

Q: What is the Blessed Trinity?

A: The Blessed Trinity is God the Father, God the Son, and God the Holy Spirit. The Blessed Trinity is the Three Persons in One God. *CCC,* 254

Q: Who were the Apostles?

A: The Apostles were twelve men Jesus chose to be the leaders of his disciples. *CCC,* 858

CCC = Catechism of the Catholic Church

Q: What is Pentecost?

A: Pentecost is the day the Holy Spirit came to the disciples. On Pentecost the Church began. *CCC, 767, 1076*

Q: What is the Church?

A: The Church is all the people who are baptized in Jesus Christ and follow his teachings. *CCC, 752, 759*

Q: What is a sacrament?

A: A sacrament is a special sign given to us by Jesus. *CCC, 1131*

Q: What is Original Sin?

A: Original Sin is the first sin which was committed when the first man and first woman disobeyed God. We are all born with Original Sin. *CCC, 404*

Q: What happens in the Sacrament of Baptism?

A: At Baptism God gives us new life. We are freed from Original Sin and all other sin and given grace, a share in God's life. *CCC, 1212, 1213*

Q: What happens in the Sacrament of Confirmation?

A: In Confirmation we are strengthened and sealed with the Gift of the Holy Spirit. *CCC, 1303*

Q: What seasons make up the Church year?

A: The seasons of the Church year are: Advent, Christmas, Lent, the Three Days, and Ordinary Time. *CCC, 1168, 1173*

Q: What do we celebrate during Ordinary Time?

A: In Ordinary Time we celebrate Jesus Christ's whole life, his Death, and his Resurrection. *CCC, 1163, 1168, 1172–1173*

Q: What is the Bible?

A: The Bible is the book of God's Word. It has two parts: the Old Testament and the New Testament. *CCC, 104, 120*

Q: What are the Gospels?

A: The Gospels are four books in the New Testament about Jesus' teachings and his life on earth. *CCC, 125*

Q: What are the Ten Commandments?

A: The Ten Commandments are the ten special laws God gave to his people. *CCC, 2058*

Q: What is the Great Commandment?

A: The Great Commandment is Jesus' teaching to love God and others. *CCC, 2055*

Q: What is free will?

A: Free will is God's gift to us that allows us to make choices. *CCC, 1730–1731*

Q: What is sin?

A: Sin is a thought, word, or act that we freely choose to commit even though we know that it is wrong. *CCC, 1850*

Q: What is the difference between mortal and venial sin?

A: Mortal sins are very serious and break our friendship with God. Venial sins are less serious and hurt our friendship with God. *CCC, 1855*

Q: **What is the Sacrament of Penance and Reconciliation?**

A: The Sacrament of Penance and Reconciliation is the sacrament in which we receive and celebrate God's forgiveness of our sins. *CCC, 1422, 1440*

Q: **What is conscience?**

A: Conscience is a gift from God that helps us know right from wrong. *CCC, 1776–1778*

Q: **What are the steps that are always part of the Sacrament of Penance and Reconciliation?**

A: The steps are: contrition, confession, penance, and absolution. *CCC, 1448*

Q: **What is Advent?**

A: Advent is a season of the Church year when we prepare to celebrate the coming of Jesus at Christmas. *CCC, 524*

Q: **What do we celebrate at Christmas?**

A: At Christmas we celebrate that the Son of God became man. *CCC, 1171*

Q: **What is the Eucharist?**

A: The Eucharist is the Sacrament of the Body and Blood of Christ. *CCC, 1323*

Q: **What is the Mass?**

A: The Mass is the celebration of the Eucharist. *CCC, 1382*

Q: **What is Holy Communion?**

A: Holy Communion is the Body and Blood of Christ under the appearances of bread and wine. *CCC, 1355*

Q: What are the two main parts of the Mass?

A: The two main parts of the Mass are the Liturgy of the Word and the Liturgy of the Eucharist. *CCC, 1346*

Q: What happens during the Liturgy of the Word?

A: During the Liturgy of the Word we worship God by listening to his Word, which is read from the Bible. Then together we pray the Creed and the Prayer of the Faithful. *CCC, 1346*

Q: What happens during the Liturgy of the Eucharist?

A: During the Liturgy of the Eucharist we bring forward the gifts of bread and wine, and pray the Eucharistic Prayer. By the power of the Holy Spirit and through the words and actions of the priest, the bread and wine become the Body and Blood of Christ, and we receive Jesus in Holy Communion. *CCC, 1346*

Q: What is the Blessed Sacrament?

A: The Blessed Sacrament is another name for the Eucharist. Jesus is present in the Blessed Sacrament. *CCC, 1330*

Q: What is Lent?

A: Lent is a season of the Church year when we prepare to celebrate the Resurrection of Jesus Christ. Lent begins on Ash Wednesday and lasts forty days. *CCC, 1438*

Q: What are the Three Days?

A: The Three Days is a season of the Church year which extends from Holy Thursday night to Easter Sunday night, when the Easter season begins. *CCC, 1168*

Q: What is a parish?

A: A parish is a local community of Catholics who worship and work together. *CCC, 2179*

Q: Who are the bishops?

A: Bishops are leaders of the Church who carry on the work of the Apostles. *CCC, 881, 886*

Q: Who is the pope?

A: The pope is the leader of the Church who continues the work of Saint Peter. *CCC, 882*

Q: Who are the saints?

A: The saints are the members of the Church who have died and are happy with God forever in Heaven. *CCC, 828*

Q: Why does the Church honor Mary?

A: The Church honors Mary because she is the Mother of God's Son, Jesus, and she is the greatest of saints. *CCC, 971*

Q: What is Easter?

A: Easter is a season of the Church year when we celebrate the Resurrection of Jesus Christ. *CCC, 1169*

Resources
for the Family

I n this section, you will find a treasury of resources to help build up your Catholic Identity at home, in your parish, and in the community. Learn more about key Catholic teachings from the themes of your child's *Celebrating Catholic Identity* retreats: **CREED, LITURGY & SACRAMENTS, MORALITY,** and **PRAYER**. For each theme, you will find Catholic prayers, practices, and devotions to share with those you love—and make a part of your daily lives as a Catholic family!

Family: "the place where parents pass on the faith to their children."

—Pope Francis
Apostolic Exhortation *Evangelii Gaudium,* 66

Spirituality and Your Second-Grade Child

Your second grader is at a unique stage in his or her emotional and spiritual growth. Second graders are starting to make larger connections beyond their immediate, egocentric concerns. They may respond to experiences in which they can connect with the feelings, reactions, and responses of others.

Second graders are also lively, curious, and easily distracted. They have an average attention span of seven minutes. Their attention will be sparked by a simplicity and "do-ability" that engages their natural curiosity and interest.

Second graders are usually growing in their ability to work cooperatively with others. Reinforce this growth by stressing the importance of love and mutual respect at home and beyond.*

Your second grader also has a great capacity for wonder. This is a natural foundation for a lifelong appreciation for the awesome mysteries of God. Sharing times of silence and reflection with your child—quiet moments of appreciation for God amidst the wonders of nature, or before bedtime—can help to foster your child's sense of awe for God.

*See *Catechetical Formation in Chaste Living,* United States Conference of Catholic Bishops, #1

Everlasting Life

Through his suffering, Death, and Resurrection, Jesus saved us from sin and restored us to God's life and love. Just as we believe in Jesus' Resurrection, we have hope in our own resurrection and everlasting life with Jesus Christ after we die. Pray the Nicene Creed as a family and pinpoint the words that express these beliefs.

Nicene Creed

I believe in one God,
    the Father almighty,
    maker of heaven and earth,
    of all things visible and invisible.

I believe in one Lord Jesus Christ,
    the Only Begotten Son of God,
    born of the Father before all ages.
    God from God, Light from Light,
    true God from true God,
    begotten, not made, consubstantial
        with the Father;
    through him all things were made.
    For us men and for our salvation
        he came down from heaven,
    and by the Holy Spirit
        was incarnate of the Virgin Mary,
            and became man.

For our sake he was crucified
        under Pontius Pilate,
    he suffered death and was buried,
    and rose again on the third day
        in accordance with the Scriptures.
    He ascended into heaven
        and is seated at the right hand
            of the Father.
    He will come again in glory to judge
        the living and the dead
        and his kingdom will have no end.

I believe in the Holy Spirit, the Lord,
        the giver of life,
    who proceeds from the Father and the Son,
    who with the Father and the Son is
        adored and glorified,
    who has spoken through the prophets.

I believe in one, holy, catholic
        and apostolic Church.
I confess one Baptism for the
        forgiveness of sins
and I look forward to the resurrection of the
        dead and the life of the world to come.
Amen.

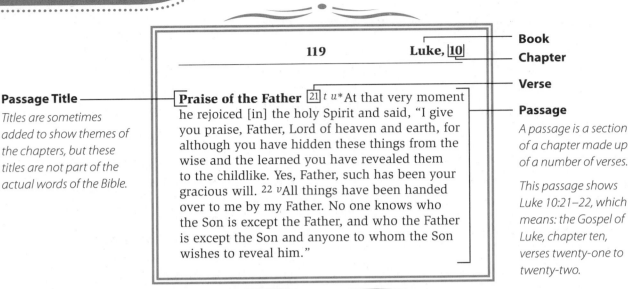

Passage Title

Titles are sometimes added to show themes of the chapters, but these titles are not part of the actual words of the Bible.

119   Luke, |10| — **Book** — **Chapter**

— **Verse**

Praise of the Father 21 *t u**At that very moment he rejoiced [in] the holy Spirit and said, "I give you praise, Father, Lord of heaven and earth, for although you have hidden these things from the wise and the learned you have revealed them to the childlike. Yes, Father, such has been your gracious will. 22 *v*All things have been handed over to me by my Father. No one knows who the Son is except the Father, and who the Father is except the Son and anyone to whom the Son wishes to reveal him."

— **Passage**

A passage is a section of a chapter made up of a number of verses.

This passage shows Luke 10:21–22, which means: the Gospel of Luke, chapter ten, verses twenty-one to twenty-two.

Reading the Bible . . . in Five Easy Steps

When you are given a Scripture passage to read, here are five easy steps that will help you to find it! With your child, follow these steps to look up **Lk 10:21–22**.

1. **Find the book.** When the name of the book is abbreviated, locate the meaning of the abbreviation on the contents pages at the beginning of your Bible. *Lk* stands for Luke, one of the four Gospels.

2. **Find the page.** Your Bible's contents pages will also show the page on which the book begins. Turn to that page within your Bible.

3. **Find the chapter.** Once you arrive at the page where the book begins, keep turning the pages forward until you find the right chapter. The image above shows you how a chapter number is usually displayed on a typical Bible page. You are looking for chapter **10** in Luke.

4. **Find the verses.** Once you find the right chapter, locate the verse or verses you need within the chapter.

The image above also shows you how verse numbers will look on a typical Bible page. You are looking for verses **21** and **22**.

5. **Start reading!**

More Than Bread and Wine

Share with your second grader that Jesus gave us the gift of the Eucharist at the Last Supper. The Eucharist is the Sacrament of the Body and Blood of Jesus Christ. Explain to your child that Jesus is really present under the appearances of bread and wine. Through the words and actions of the priest and by the power of the Holy Spirit, the bread and wine are changed and become the Body and Blood of Christ. The true presence of Jesus Christ in the Eucharist under the appearances of bread and wine is called the Real Presence.

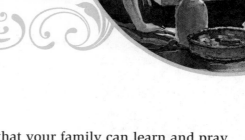

Here is a prayer before communion that your family can learn and pray when you are at Mass.

Prayer Before Communion

O God, who in this wonderful Sacrament left us a memorial of your Passion: grant, we implore you, that we may so venerate the sacred mysteries of your Body and Blood, as always to be conscious of the fruit of your redemption. You who live and reign forever and ever.

Amen.

(From *Tantum Ergo*)

Celebrating All Year

Talk with your child about the meaning of liturgy. The liturgy is the official public prayer of the Church. This includes the Mass, Liturgy of the Hours, and all the celebrations of the sacraments. In the liturgy we gather as a community joined to Christ to celebrate what we believe.

Does your family know that the Church has its own liturgical year? In one liturgical year we recall and celebrate the whole life of Jesus Christ. The liturgical year begins in late November or early December with the season of Advent. It includes such seasons and feasts as Christmas, Lent, Easter, and Pentecost Sunday.

Holy Days of Obligation

Each Sunday of the liturgical year is a great celebration of the Church, or a solemnity. In addition to each Sunday, there are other solemnities in the liturgical year on which we are obliged to attend Mass to give special honor to Jesus Christ for the salvation he has given to us. These are called Holy Days of Obligation. Post this list of holy days in the home to remind everyone of them!

- **Solemnity of Mary, Mother of God (January 1)**
- **Ascension (when celebrated on Thursday during the Easter season*)**
- **Assumption of Mary (August 15)**
- **All Saints' Day (November 1)**
- **Immaculate Conception (December 8)**
- **Christmas (December 25)**

* Some dioceses celebrate the Ascension on the following Sunday.

Seven Themes of Catholic Social Teaching

Human dignity is the value and worth that come from being created in God's image and likeness. Throughout Jesus' life and teaching, he stood up for the human dignity of every person. Jesus' life and teaching are the foundation of Catholic social teaching. This teaching calls us to work for justice and peace as Jesus did. Discuss with your family ways in which you can work together for justice and peace.

1. **Life and Dignity of the Human Person** Human life is sacred because it is a gift from God. Because we are all God's children, we all share the same human dignity. As Christians we respect all people, even those we do not know.

2. **Call to Family, Community, and Participation** We are all social. We need to be with others to grow. The family is the basic community. In the family we grow and learn the values of our faith. As Christians we live those values in our family and community.

3. **Rights and Responsibilities of the Human Person** Every person has a fundamental right to life. This includes the things we need to have a decent life: faith and family, work and education, health care and housing. We also have a responsibility to others and to society. We work to make sure the rights of all people are being protected.

4. **Option for the Poor and Vulnerable** We have a special obligation to help those who are poor and in need. This includes those who cannot protect themselves because of their age or their health.

5. **Dignity of Work and the Rights of Workers** Our work is a sign of our participation in God's work. People have the right to decent work, just wages, safe working conditions, and to participate in decisions about work.

6. **Solidarity of the Human Family** Solidarity is a feeling of unity. It binds members of a group together. Each of us is a member of the one human family. The human family includes people of all racial and cultural backgrounds. We all suffer when one part of the human family suffers whether they live near or far away.

7. **Care for God's Creation** God created us to be stewards, or caretakers, of his creation. We must care for and respect the environment. We have to protect it for future generations. When we care for creation, we show respect for God the Creator.

A Roadmap to Happiness

What makes your family happy? When we live as Jesus' disciples, we can find true happiness. The Beatitudes are Jesus' teachings that describe the way to live as his disciples. In the Beatitudes the word *blessed* means "happy."

The Beatitudes	What the Beatitudes Mean for Us
"Blessed are the poor in spirit, for theirs is the kingdom of heaven."	We are "poor in spirit" when we depend on God and make God more important than anyone or anything else in our lives.
"Blessed are they who mourn, for they will be comforted."	We "mourn" when we are sad because of the selfish ways people treat each other.
"Blessed are the meek, for they will inherit the land."	We are "meek" when we are patient, kind, and respectful to all people, even those who do not respect us.
"Blessed are they who hunger and thirst for righteousness, for they will be satisfied."	We "hunger and thirst for righteousness" when we search for justice and treat everyone fairly.
"Blessed are the merciful, for they will be shown mercy."	We are "merciful" when we forgive others and do not take revenge on those who hurt us.
"Blessed are the clean of heart, for they will see God."	We are "clean of heart" when we are faithful to God's teachings and try to see God in all people and all situations.
"Blessed are the peacemakers, for they will be called children of God."	We are "peacemakers" when we treat others with love and respect and when we help others to stop fighting and make peace.
"Blessed are they who are persecuted for the sake of righteousness, for theirs is the kingdom of heaven." Matthew 5:3–10	We are "persecuted for the sake of righteousness" when others disrespect us for living as disciples of Jesus and following his example.

What Are Sacramentals?

Are there any sacramentals, such as rosaries, around your home? Sacramentals are those blessings, actions, and objects that help us respond to God's grace received in the sacraments. Here are some examples:

- blessings of people, places, foods, and objects

- objects such as rosaries, medals, crucifixes, blessed ashes, and blessed palms

- actions such as making the Sign of the Cross, sprinkling holy water, or praying the Stations of the Cross.

Stations of the Cross

Did your family know that the Stations of the Cross are among the oldest ways of honoring the events of Jesus' life, suffering, Death, and Resurrection?

Your family may have seen the Stations of the Cross depicted along walls of your parish church. If possible, pray the stations together as a family. Here's how:

At each station, stop and remember one of these events:

1. Jesus is condemned to die.
2. Jesus takes up his cross.
3. Jesus falls the first time.
4. Jesus meets his mother.
5. Simon helps Jesus carry his cross.
6. Veronica wipes the face of Jesus.
7. Jesus falls the second time.
8. Jesus meets the women of Jerusalem.
9. Jesus falls the third time.
10. Jesus is stripped of his garments.
11. Jesus is nailed to the cross.
12. Jesus dies on the cross.
13. Jesus is taken down from the cross.
14. Jesus is laid in the tomb.

Then

PRAY

✝ We adore you, O Christ,
and we bless you.
Because by your holy cross,
you have redeemed the world.

A Virtuous Life

Explain to your child that a virtue is a good habit that helps us to act according to God's plan for us. The virtues of faith, hope, and love (also called charity) are theological virtues. Virtues help guide our conduct with the help of God's grace.

An Act of Faith

O God, we believe in all that Jesus has taught us about you.
We place all our trust in you because of your great love for us.

An Act of Hope

O God, we never give up on your love.
We have hope and will work for your kingdom to come and for a life that lasts forever with you in heaven.

An Act of Love

O God, we love you above all things.
Help us to love ourselves and one another as Jesus taught us to do.